She, He, They

'*She, He, They* is an open and honest account of the perspective of a parent of a trans/non-binary young person coming out. It challenges us to think seriously about the need to provide greater support for parents and families, during what is a critical and difficult time. It speaks about the combination of gender identity and disability and it is the intersections of people's lived-experience that often go unrecognised. The reader is given the chance to share in one family's journey towards being comfortable with its diversity and common human experience.'
Fergus McMillan, Chief Executive, LGBT Youth Scotland

'*She, He, They* is an intimate look at what happens to a family when a child comes out as transgender. Insightful, moving and refreshingly honest, Shirley Young tackles an often emotive subject head on, and the final product is a gentle, warm and considered exploration of trans issues from a parent's point of view. Essential reading, Young's book gives readers a window into what it means to transition from female to male whilst also detailing her own emotional transition as she learns to face up to her feelings of grief and loss.'   **Carrie Lyell, DIVA magazine**

'This book is a raw, honest and heartfelt account of the response of one family to the bombshell news of their child's transition from female to male to non-binary. The fall-out from such news can have ripples which may not be anticipated and can rock the world of all in contact. Shirley examines her feelings about what happened in a way with which many will identify.'
Founder parent, TransparenTsees

She, He, They

Families, gender and coping with transition

Shirley Young

C|C|W|B press

First published by CCWB Press in 2016
Reprinted 2021
Centre for Confidence and Well-being.
Registered Office Abercorn House,
79 Renfrew Rd, Paisley, PA3 4DA

**A catalogue record of this book is available
from the British Library**
978-0-9933527-3-7

Printed and bound in Great Britain by
Bell & Bain Ltd, Glasgow.

POSTCARDS FROM SCOTLAND

Series editor: Carol Craig

Advisory group:
Professor Phil Hanlon, Chair,
Centre for Confidence and Well-being;
Fred Shedden

CONTENTS

FOREWORD

'It's been worse than finding out they are disabled.
It's worse than if she had died – at least then we
could have had a funeral and people would have
understood our grief and loss.
We would have been given support.'

My husband Ian and I made these statements when our
daughter told us, aged 20, that she needed to become a man.
Eleven years into this journey of acknowledging, adjusting
and adapting to our son's identity, I hope our story might be
useful for those going through a similar experience. It may
also help those who support families professionally as well
as relations, friends, work colleagues and acquaintances of
those going through this process of profound change.

In this book I hope to to give readers insight into what it
feels like to have all one understands about gender and
identity challenged. I explore how my own background and
my husband's affected our family's coping strategies. I also
reflect on the challenges and rewards that we have so far
experienced as a family.

I consider how the external environment – social, economic

and political, in Scotland, the UK and globally, has affected our experiences over the past eleven years.

I passionately believe that every family is unique and that if families are to be supported effectively then that uniqueness, the set of circumstances that have shaped their experiences, will influence their responses to the reality of their child's identity. Given this, how can a person who is gender variant and their family be supported? How can those who support them ensure that their own prejudices and stereotypes do not negatively affect the support they provide?

These are the questions I try to answer in this book. Through the narratives of each member in our family and the people around us, as well as stories shared with me by other families, I offer some suggestions and raise questions for the future. Various terms I use throughout the book may not be familiar to some readers so in Chapter 7 I provide definitions which you may find helpful.

CHAPTER 1
'I need to be a man . . .'

The night I lost my beautiful, fine-boned, pixie-faced, blue-eyed, lesbian daughter there was no ambulance whisking her to A & E, no sad-eyed police constables with suitably arranged facial expressions at the door to break the bad news of her passing. Nor was there a kindly consultant saying they tried everything, but sadly she was no more. There was just, in the silence of midnight, the simple statement, spoken in an agony of fear and trepidation – 'I need to be a man mum. I *am* a man.'

We had had such a lovely evening. It was Jane's twentieth birthday and much to my surprise and delight, she wanted to spend it with me and my all-female staff team at a favourite Italian restaurant. My husband and son were excluded from this big girls' night out to mark the end of her teenage years. She had just returned home after a year working as a volunteer support worker at our disabled son Colin's former residential special school in the south of England. Colin had moved to the sixth form college there and they had both come home at the end of term a few days previously.

The prosecco flowed and it was great fun. At least it was for us – a view probably not shared by other diners. At one point in the evening, the team presented Jane with bright pink underwear, which she gamefully held up for all to admire. I was in my element. This is exactly what I had imagined life with my adult daughter would be like, with a ready-made best friend who I loved more than life itself. I felt so privileged because we hadn't always had an easy relationship when she was younger, but those issues had been resolved. I saw the rest of our lives stretching ahead of us where we would be each other's confidante, companion on holidays and I would hopefully one day be a much-loved mother-in-law to her female life partner and granny to their children.

I had however been shocked at her appearance when she returned home a couple of days before. She had shorn off her trademark heavily waxed, spiky black hair with pink or purple tips and replaced her short skirt, black tights and Doc Marten boots with camouflage combats and t-shirt. I had seen her go through various styles over the years and thought she was having a butch phase, perhaps to please a current love interest. Although I personally didn't find it a very appealing look, I didn't think too much about it. In retrospect I can see that subconsciously I did not want to acknowledge what it might mean.

Jane had seemed troubled for the past couple of years. This was in spite of her apparently very happy relationship with her schoolgirl sweetheart Cara and her obvious enjoyment of her drama course. She had developed an eating disorder when she was 14 and this had got worse lately. I had noticed more and more fine scars on her arms which I suspected were as a result of her self-harming.

Ian and I had struggled with her behaviour all the time she was growing up. Professionals told us it was attention-seeking due to the fact that we had to devote much of our time and energy supporting and carrying out various therapies with our son Colin, who has cerebral palsy. This made some sense, but did not seem to fully explain why Jane didn't appear to want to please us, challenged every single request and whenever was told off for misbehaving wailed, 'but I don't understand what I've done wrong'. We thought she was just saying that as an excuse but, as it transpired, it was the truth. Sadly, Jane 'acted out' whenever there was a change, often turning what we had expected would please her – a surprise or going on holiday, for example – into a battleground. This meant that Jane had become the scapegoat for all the family's distress. To our shame and regret Ian and I were on occasion extremely harsh in our treatment of her. When she moved to secondary school, where she was struggling with the written work despite her high level verbal skills, I asked for an educational psychologist's assessment for her and also for a referral to the child and adolescent mental health team.

At that time I was Director of the Special Needs Information Point (SNIP), an information, advice and support service for parents of sick and disabled children at the Royal Hospital for Sick Children in Edinburgh. (It is now known as Kindred.) I therefore had some knowledge about specific learning difficulties as they were then described and our rights under education legislation, and I suspected there was more to Jane's learning issues than was being acknowledged by the school.

This knowledge was extremely useful as it enabled me, at last, to get Jane assessed and access some of the help and support she needed. When Jane was 12 a senior educational psychologist finally identified that she had a range of developmental conditions, including dyslexia and dyscalculia. A consultant paediatrician referral followed and she diagnosed Jane with Gerstmann's Syndrome. These conditions meant she had an inability to recognise faces, to navigate around unfamiliar places and to process language or number. They also made her take things literally, much like someone on the autistic spectrum, and meant she was unable to learn incidentally. Although her verbal reasoning was calculated to be that of an 18 year old, her spelling age was 7 and her maths age 6! The educational psychologist said he was so impressed that she had persisted with school because many children with these conditions truant. Undoubtedly this degree of disparity between her abilities must have been causing her a great deal of stress.

These developmental impairments meant that for much of Jane's childhood she did not know what was going on around her, couldn't find her way about and struggled to make sense of social situations. It was heartbreaking for Ian and me to hear that in early primary school she had been so terrified of me leaving her because she couldn't find her way from the classroom to the toilets. She practically stopped eating her lunch because she struggled to manage tray, food and money and one day had dropped it all. To overcome this she resorted to just having one sausage each day so that there was less chance of it ending up on the floor.

As a result of her learning problems she was seen as 'different' and experienced bullying at school. We now understand that trying to behave well there and to protect us from finding out that our 'perfect' child also had impairments, albeit invisible ones, was a daily challenge for her. What we experienced at home was the venting of her frustration and anger. In addition to her learning difficulties, Jane had also developed severe asthma at 10, which resulted in numerous visits to A & E. Her hypermobile joints, which started to give her a lot of pain around the same time, developed into juvenile arthritis. This was eventually diagnosed when she was 14 and resulted in her using either crutches or, when it was really painful, a wheelchair to get around. Each time there was a new diagnosis we thought 'this was it'. Finally we had an explanation for her 'difference' and why she never seemed to feel happy and content within herself.

Of course we now understand that added to this mix was gender dysphoria. Her gender identity did not match with her sex characteristics, causing her great aversion to and discomfort with her body, in particular her breasts. We now realise how some of her discomfort around wearing her school pinafore was not just that she was 'tactile defensive', i.e. that she found certain textures impossible to tolerate against her skin due to her impairments, but also because she couldn't understand why we insisted in putting her in girl's clothes when she was a boy!

Another of her common phrases that we found bewildering was 'What will people think?' whenever she was dressed in her skating tutu or her Brownie uniform and about to get out of the car and go into a shop. I would always respond with a chuckle – 'They will think you've just been skating or to Brownies', and thought it just one of her foibles not understanding it was far from superficial for her and causing her a great deal of distress. Jane knew that something was wrong but wasn't able to articulate it so every morning before primary school was a battleground. Jane protested against putting on her uniform pinafore dress and would wail that she had 'the wrong pants on'.

Alongside this issue with clothes, Jane was obsessed with watching the TV series *London's Burning*. When I asked her why she loved it so much she would respond that she wanted to become a fireman when she grew up. Full of my feminist righteousness I would remind her that the term she was looking for was 'firefighter'. Of course we now see it was not the profession but the gender she was aspiring to.

Thankfully the various diagnoses of her learning disabilities forced us to shift our attitudes and behaviour towards our lovely, misunderstood daughter. The conflict between us resolved very quickly, but her relationship with her father, Ian, remained volatile at times.

It was this volatility and aggressive behaviour towards Ian that was the catalyst for her coming out as transgender the night of her birthday. When we rolled loudly into the living room Ian was watching TV and, without asking, Jane picked up the remote control and started channel hopping. Ian was understandably annoyed and before I knew it they were having a full-blown argument.

Ian stormed off to bed and I asked her why she behaved so aggressively towards her dad. This is what forced her to disclose that her life had been hell; she was trapped in, as she understood it at the time, the wrong body, which she hated. She told me that if it hadn't been for a therapist she had been seeing down in England who persuaded her not to kill herself or go missing she would not have come home.

Any annoyance I had been experiencing dissolved and I was full of compassion and concern for her. I listened as she described, that from around the age of 15, when she started to attend a young people's group with her girlfriend at the wonderful LGBT Youth Scotland, she had found an explanation for her feelings of discomfort and distress about her female body. The bandages I had seen in her underwear drawer over the past few years, which I had thought were for her often sprained ankles and wrists due to her hypermobile joints, were what she had been using to bind herself to acquire a flat chest.

As the truth came out I remembered with shame her asking me to sit with her and watch *Boys Don't Cry* – a harrowing film about a trans young person. I fell asleep half way through, after pronouncing how glad I was that she was 'just lesbian' as the transgender life portrayed in the film was so hard to watch. She went on to tell me that she had been accepted as male in clubs she had been attending in England for the past few months and that had felt so good.

Relieved that she had felt able to tell me and that she had not committed suicide I bid her goodnight. I also told her, as I had every day of her life, that I loved her. I then went to bed to break the news to Ian.

Background to our story

To say that I had adored having a daughter was an understatement. Before Jane was born I only really wanted a daughter. After I gave birth to our second child, I was thrilled to have the 'perfect' one of each.

I had had a challenging upbringing, living in poverty with an oppressive and violent dad who I now understand had suffered from Post Traumatic Stress Disorder. This was due to his experiences both as the black sheep of the family, having what I now understand were Attention Deficit Hyperactivity Disorder (ADHD) and dyslexia-type difficulties and to his very traumatic time spent as a machine gunner in World War II. As a child my mum had been the victim of violence from her mother's partner. This had resulted in this man and my grandmother being imprisoned for child cruelty. Mum had been physically frail all her life as she had suffered from rheumatic fever which left her with a damaged heart. She had a miscarriage and a stillborn birth prior to delivering her first healthy baby, my brother Terry, followed within thirteen months by my sister Pat. I was born eleven years later, after mum had had open-heart surgery to replace leaking valves. When I was 10, mum developed severe paranoid schizophrenia and attempted suicide on a couple of occasions, probably due to inappropriate drug treatment for her anxiety.

These experiences had left me ambivalent about men and yearning to create the family I had craved for myself growing up. I had seen glimpses of these families in books, on television programmes and in the lives of some of the women I had attached myself to – mainly teachers and Guide Leaders – families headed up by strong, feisty women who I believed were not dominated by men.

Ian had also wanted a daughter. He had a fantasy that as an adult woman she would surprise him by turning up at his workplace to take him out for lunch. After Colin was born he was equally delighted to have a son, although again he had no real expectations of what that would mean, other than he hoped they would play football together. He now thinks that he was quite gender-blind when the children were growing up – treating them both as little people, rather than reinforcing gender stereotypes. He didn't expect Jane to express femininity through particular styles of dress or behaviour. Ian's mum did not wear skirts or dresses and played the mouth organ and spoons, so his ideas of femininity were fairly well removed from the stereotypes of the time. Equally, Ian did not identify as 'alpha male' and to this day prefers the company of women or similarly gentle men. He was delighted when at the Science Festival Jane showed an aptitude for soldering. Equally he had no problem when Colin aged 3 asked for a baby doll, complete with changes of clothes and feeding set for his Christmas.

Ian freely admits he has always been more interested in what he himself is doing than in anyone else's life and this has both helped and hindered his parenting of our children. He has been able to be more objective than I ever was and better at giving them space to be themselves. But when they were little he was sometimes distant and unengaged, far preferring to spend every hour at work or playing football than being at home. None of this is surprising given his upbringing, with a father who was similarly absent and deep, persistent cultural expectations that mums look after the children and dads provide. In addition, Ian had been very ill as a child and had also been involved in a road traffic accident which resulted in two lengthy stays in hospital. At that time parents were not able to stay overnight with their children. It was through therapy I came to understand that his anger when I got home each evening from an extended stay at our child's bedside was triggered by his own feelings of abandonment as a child. If only I had understood this at the time it would have saved us from a lot of added distress when our children were ill in hospital.

As a teenager, I had been a bugler in a Scout and Guide Band and enjoyed feeling equal to the boys. It therefore felt natural to escape poverty by following my brother into the Royal Navy after leaving school at 17. He was by then a Sub-Lieutenant, having gained his commission after rising through the ranks. He had been a positive role model for me whilst I was growing up. My schoolwork had been compromised due to my caring role for mum, but thanks to supportive teaching staff, in particular Sandra Hodgkins and Molly Douglass, I managed to get five O Grades – enough to allow me to become a WRNS Officer. My aptitude tests showed I was capable of a highly technical role and I was delighted to do a job similar to that of the men at sea – Radar Plotter. It was the 1970s and I relished pushing the boundaries of what men thought women could do. I had no intentions of settling down until well into my twenties, once I had established my naval career. However once I was in the Royal Navy I did not find the realities of the Officers' Mess appealing. Since I was still seeking the love and security that had been denied to me when I was growing up, I abandoned my planned officer training at the age of 19 when I met Ian at the disco in the NAAFI bar. I was 20 and Ian 21 when we got married and started to live in married quarters. We decided we wanted to be settled and secure before we embarked on parenthood and so left the navy and moved to Edinburgh where Ian had grown up. I started to work in a building society and Ian got a job with an office machinery company.

All through this time I had been a Guide Leader, running a weekly unit and then also becoming a trainer, delivering courses all over Scotland for other Guiders. This devotion to Guiding had arisen out of the fantastic support my Guide leaders had given me when I was a girl, letting me go to camp for free when mum was in hospital, knowing that my dad could not afford to pay. I loved working with the girls and was more than happy to give up my time, wanting to 'give something back' to the organisation that had been such a supportive one to me as a girl.

It's a girl! (apparently)

I became pregnant when I was 27 and Ian 29. In retrospect, given our backgrounds and our lack of support systems, we were probably not best placed to become parents. Both our fathers had died in their fifties due to smoking related illnesses and we had mothers who were emotionally, and in Ian's case, physically dependent on us. They were only 54 and 64, but looked and seemed two decades older. Once again this was due to the hard lives they had lived in poverty. They had both coped by smoking and Ian's mother also used drink to survive. She had also been the victim of her stepmother's violence when she was growing up. A break-in after her divorce had ruined her confidence and she subsequently developed agoraphobia.

Despite all these problems in our own past, I was determined to create my 'perfect' family. Yes it was true that my own sister, and closest family member, was four hundred miles away but I had been living away from home for ten years.

Besides, I had a wide circle of friends and was supremely confident that my kind, gentle, caring husband was the perfect father for my children – a father who would be involved in their upbringing and as interested as me in their development. This assumption was based on seeing him briefly with his friends' children for whom he babysat occasionally. He also loved cooing over babies.

Jane's delivery was hugely traumatic as after being in the breech position she had turned 'the wrong way', meaning a prolonged and excruciating 'backache' labour which lasted forty-eight hours. Jane didn't cry when she finally emerged and the nurses rushed her away to get suctioned. However, they returned her to me almost immediately as she started screaming halfway down the corridor. We were ecstatic and I felt like the queen. I had done it! I had the daughter I had longed for and everything in my world was perfect. I am embarrassed to admit that I felt so superior to the women who just had boys. I had my mini-me and through her I would relive my own life and give her everything that had been lacking in mine. What could possibly go wrong? The trauma of the birth kept me awake for another 48 hours. I was suffering terrible flashbacks and in between gazing adoringly at my beautiful daughter I felt like I was falling. Jane breastfed well but hated being wrapped up. Whilst all the other babies cried when their clothing and nappies came off, she did the opposite, thrashing around and managing to get everything off her skin to the point she had to be taken away to be warmed up. Unbeknown to us this was the first sign that our perfect baby might have some problems.

As I recovered from the birth I quickly decided that if I

didn't have another baby fairly soon I wouldn't have the courage to go through it all again! Jane's first Christmas came and with it my first dawning that Ian and I had markedly different expectations of parenting. His work's festive lunch was on Christmas Eve and I was so excited about him coming home so that we could wrap Jane's presents together and hang her stocking up on her cot. I had not actually shared that plan with him; I just assumed he would be as interested as me to do this. He finally came home at 1 am on Christmas Day. There were no mobile phones in those days and by the time he returned I oscillated between fear that he had been killed and anger that he wasn't home. With the benefit of counselling, I now understand his lack of interest in being with me for our daughter's first Christmas Eve had triggered painful childhood memories: my mother's virtual absence as she sat with a blank face not knowing who I was or muttering about Russian spies talking to her through the radio, as well as waiting for my brother and sister to come for Christmas and them not appearing. I had suffered terrible feelings of abandonment in my past but I could not talk about them, as I had been so successful at blocking them out. Understandably Ian could not understand why I was so distressed. Photographs of our first Christmas as parents show me baggy eyed and exhausted from crying.

This incident precipitated a downward spiral into full-blown postnatal depression, although I didn't know this was the case at the time. Ian expected me to be happy because I had the baby I wanted and I was feeling more and more inept. She was not interested in solid food. When all my friend's babies were tucking into jars of food, Jane was firmly turning her face away from meals I had cooked from scratch for her.

All the skills that had made me an effective manager and Guide Leader could not help me cope with this baby who wanted to breastfeed every minute of the day. Everyday tasks I had once found easy became impossible to achieve, sending me into paroxysms of grief out of all proportion to the problem.

Gradually, when Jane was a year old, things began to ease. I told the Health Visitor about her lack of interest in solid food. She weighed Jane and found she was only the same weight at a year as three months earlier. She recommended I recommence full-time breastfeeding, which was actually easier than trying to spoon-feed her. As soon as I started giving her food she could pick up with her hands she began eating a variety of solids. We now know her aversion to being spoon-fed was because she could not judge the speed of the spoon coming towards her. She found this frightening and so turned her head away.

With her development now apparently back to normal I started to believe again that I could do this 'mothering thing'. We had become a little team and I started to really enjoy Jane's company, taking her for her first picnic to Edinburgh's Botanical Gardens and to a toddler group where everyone thought she was such a cutie with her blonde hair and pixie face. I was so proud of her and her quirky ways – she bottom shuffled, just as I had done, while every other child crawled. She was easily frightened though and after being pushed over by some of the bigger children became somewhat child-phobic demanding to be picked up if another toddler walked towards her.

Meanwhile, Ian was working extremely hard and loving every minute of it. He left home early in the morning and rarely returned until after six, but was usually home in time to give Jane her bath and read from her favourite story.

When Jane was fifteen months we were delighted to discover I was pregnant again. I so wanted a second child so that she would not be lonely like I had been, living on my own with my older parents. Ian also thought it would be nice for her to have a brother or sister. Our two mums were thrilled when we gave them each a tiny bootee for Christmas with a label saying 'You don't know me yet, but I am your future grand-child – I'll have these back when I am born in the summer'. Sadly, my mum was never to meet our much-wanted second baby. Five weeks before my due date, the day before my 29th birthday, she died of a major stroke.

Jane entered the terrible twos by the time she was 18 months. Talking in sentences, able to say her name, address and telephone number when the other toddlers were saying 'car' and 'dadda' she was incredibly bright and the other mums expressed envy. But for me, heavily pregnant and with no extended family support, her constant demands were starting to wear me down. In a precursor of what was to follow, she argued over everything she was asked to do and was forever taking her clothes off. I remember wondering, a few days after my due date had passed, how on earth I was going to look after a newborn baby and this child who wanted me to play with her *all* the time. The only way I managed to get a lie down was to play hairdressers or doctors!

Another traumatic birth

Early on a Saturday morning, six days after my due date, I went into labour. After my previous experience of spending two days in hospital before Jane was delivered, I resisted going in for as long as possible. When my contractions were every ten minutes Ian insisted and we arrived just in time for me to go straight to the delivery suite. I described my previous labour and the staff decided to break my waters. This caused my labour to accelerate very quickly and within a few minutes I needed to push. I remember the atmosphere in the delivery room being wonderful – very relaxed with a lot of laughing. I was using gas and air so effectively this time, with the baby the right way round and I was really proud of myself, having the delivery I had felt I had failed at previously.

All this would change, however, when the baby, delivered onto my tummy as Ian had requested, lay pale blue, flat and not breathing. Then all hell broke loose as the midwife hastily cut the cord and snatched our beautiful baby boy away from us to be resuscitated. Still euphoric from the delivery and gas and air, I convinced myself that just like they had with Jane, they would bring him back to us soon. As the minutes ticked by I said 'they must be cleaning him up for us' but the fear in the room was starting to become palpable. The poor student midwife didn't know what to say and we were starting to panic, when the senior midwife returned to say that our baby was very sick and a doctor was coming from another hospital with a ventilating incubator to take him to the special care baby unit. That was the first I understood that the low-tech birth I had chosen meant there was no ventilator available for this kind of emergency.

The ambulance arrived. They brought him to see us briefly and asked if we wanted to go with him to the other hospital. There was no room in the ambulance, so within an hour or so of giving birth, Ian was driving me in our own car across Edinburgh, with a student nurse as the only support should I develop any complications from the delivery. I now appreciate how dangerous this was, but at the time the shock and aftermath of giving birth to this very sick baby meant I was in no position to remonstrate with the staff and demand a second ambulance.

We were put in a side ward and told that someone would come and get us to visit our new baby once he was settled into the special care baby unit. We sat alone for around three hours, not knowing if he was dead or alive. At around four in the morning we were told we could go and see him and asked if there was anyone we could call for support. Instead of getting Ian to ring my sister so far away, or Ian's mum who was so frail, I asked him to contact my lovely friend Jean Brown, who I was close to through Girl Guiding. Ian, still in tears, rang Jean. All she heard was that he needed her, not knowing whether it was me who had died or something to do with the baby. By the time Jean arrived, we had been given the heartbreaking news it was unlikely our baby would survive. We arranged to get him christened and decided to call him Colin. Everyone but the chaplain, including the doctors and nurses, cried as this little boy, whose face was covered in bandages to hold the ventilator pipe in place, was baptised, with a little bunch of flowers on the top of the incubator. We had not seen his eyes, did not know the colour of his hair or how much he weighed but we loved him fiercely.

On day two Ian and I felt so much pain as we watched Colin in agony. Whilst the doctors took blood from his tiny feet every fifteen minutes to check the blood gases, we would have switched the ventilator off and let him slip away had we been given the choice. Thank goodness we didn't, because Colin was a fighter and within another two days had confounded the medics by breathing for himself and pulling through.

Colin was still very poorly though and in and out of hospital for the next two years. Jane would come into our bedroom in the morning, sucking her thumb, to peer into her baby brother's little wooden cradle, only to find it empty. This was very distressing for her and she would cry for him.

On the surface I was managing well, but a second traumatic delivery so soon after the death of my mother, coupled with caring for a sick baby and a toddler who had all these hidden impairments, took its toll and I suffered another bout of postnatal depression. This time I was able to access some therapeutic support and gradually made another full recovery. Ian also realised that he needed to be around more to support me in parenting our young children and stopped working such long hours.

Early childhood onwards

Over the next few years it became apparent that Colin had suffered brain damage at birth and by the age of 4 he was a wheelchair user. His needs were so pronounced and visible that they masked Jane's difficulties. The two of them got on really well though and would spend hours playing Jane's made-up games, in which I now understand Colin had no problem with her playing male roles. As a feminist I thought nothing of her wandering around the house in red pants as Mowgli to Colin's Baloo and was delighted that my daughter defied gender stereotypes in her play.

However I enjoyed our girlie Saturdays, when she and I went ice-skating. I first took her at the age of 4 and she took to it like a duck to water. Within weeks she had her first tutu and was skating around the rink grand-style. We arranged lessons for her and were told she had the potential to be a champion. In reality however her sequencing difficulties would mean that she would be unable to memorise a programme. But she pursued this hobby for about six years, until numerous injuries and her developing arthritis curtailed it. I had loved being a skater-mum, making sure she was on the ice for 8am during the school holidays. It was our thing that we had separate from Colin and his needs and we both felt its loss. Little did I know that Jane's request to stay and watch the boys playing ice hockey was because it was that sport, rather than figure skating, she hankered for.

As she entered her teenage years it became obvious that Jane had inherited my family's musical gene and by the age of 15 was studying oboe and piano at the prestigious City of Edinburgh Music Unit, based at Broughton High School.

Ian remembers her at this time 'lighting up a room, beautiful and sparkly, clever and talented'. He was so proud to attend her various concerts. Not being musical himself he was overawed by her ability to pick up an instrument and play it by ear. That secondary school and the unit were the making of Jane. The Head of Learning Support, Moira Thomson, quickly identified how bright she was and ensured she met her academic potential. The unit also provided a haven during break times. As someone with compromised social skills and gender issues, Jane had found the playground with all its attendant 'unspoken rules' and gender norms, extremely difficult to navigate. Sadly this same school could not provide what Colin needed. He really missed having a wheelchair-using peer group. Although we tried to enable this by taking him to sporting events, which he loved and proved successful at, by the time he was 12 he was expressing great distress. In addition, I was struggling to scribe for him and Jane every night. It was taking about four hours to do their homework and Ian didn't feel he had the skills to help with this. Things got to crisis point and it was with heavy hearts that we arranged for Colin to move to a residential special school in Hampshire. We had visited a few years previously and knew it would offer him what he was looking for, but it was still not what we would have chosen, knowing we would miss him so much.

Broken dreams

It was in the context of all of this history that Jane dropped her bombshell. As a family we had already had so much trauma, grief and loss in our lives. Ian and I had just got to the point of feeling we had adjusted and adapted well to the reality of having two disabled young adult children and were starting to relax and have fun.

Colin was going to go to Loughborough University to study politics and social policy after the summer and Jane was applying to study occupational therapy back in Edinburgh, once again living at home. I was delighted to be achieving my dream of Jane and myself developing the mutually supportive mother/adult daughter relationship I had been denied with my own mother. In addition, over the years my own sexual identity had also shifted. Happily married for over thirty years and considering myself heterosexual, much to my surprise I had developed a deep emotional and physical (non-reciprocated) attraction to another woman and discovered that I was bisexual. I shared this revelation with Ian and he was brilliant, telling me that I only had one life and if I needed to leave him for a female partner, then I must do so, as he loved me enough to let me be who I needed to be. This expression of unconditional love affirmed for me that he was absolutely the person I wanted to share the rest of my life with. I continue to be so impressed with the way he dealt with my disclosure. The thought that I had this attraction to women in common with Jane made my bond with her feel even stronger and I was looking forward to telling her about this, when in an instant all that seemed lost. Here was my feminist ally in the family suddenly telling me she needed to be a man. It felt like an enormous betrayal. I could not believe that someone who I had felt was such a great soulmate was going over to the other side and becoming a man. It felt like I was going to become a minority within the family and I had visions of the men in my family ganging up on me.

Feminism was particularly near to the surface for me at the time, not only because of my sexual identity shift, but also because working at SNIP exposed me to all the stories of mothers of disabled children whose male partners had not felt able to support them in parenting their children. The separation rate at the time for families with a disabled child was one in two. Indeed listening to story after story of absent and/or inadequate fathers had hardened my ambivalent feelings towards men. Coupled with this was a growing awareness and understanding of the continuing need for feminism. I was being appointed to increasingly high status roles within the voluntary and public sectors but there weren't as many other women there as I had expected. Nonetheless my exposure to the powerful, influential women who were there encouraged me to read feminist literature for the first time not having had the benefit of doing so at university.

So, given all of this, Jane's disclosure could not have come at a more difficult time. What's more, although I had close female friends, the relationship with my daughter had been the most precious in my life. The love I felt for Jane was something my own mother could not give or receive given her mental ill-health problems. It was also a challenge for my sister as she finds physical affection between adults uncomfortable. But I could give love to and receive love from my daughter and I cherished this fact. The news from Jane that she needed to become a man therefore felt like the ultimate rejection of what I most valued in myself – feminism, openness, warmth and affection.

We had a whole new challenge ahead of us and as I went to tell Ian about what Jane had told me I was full of anxiety about what this would do to us as a family.

The nightmare begins

Ian's response to the news was to break down in tears. As usual, tears did not come to me initially as I was in my brave, coping mode. Thankfully this did not last and I was able to cry the following evening. I rarely stopped crying for the next few months, which was both therapeutic and exhausting.

I don't think we slept much that night, not only because we were dealing with the shock of Jane's revelation, but because the following day Colin was scheduled to have surgery to replace the mechanism for feeding him through a tube in his stomach. This was going to be a particularly nerve-racking experience for us all, since the previous year when the device was first inserted he had taken a terrible reaction to the surgery. This led to him having extremely painful full body, dystonic spasms for a number of hours, during which time we had to deal with our darling 17 year old son begging us to kill him to stop the pain. Surgeons and neurologists put their heads together to work out how they could stop this situation repeating itself, but understandably we were all anxious that their plans might not work.

At some point, either during our conversation the evening before or early on the morning of Colin's operation, Jane told me that the male names she had chosen were Nathaniel Paul. Paul because that was the name we would have given our baby if it had not presented with female genitalia at birth. I was still in shock, reeling from the overwhelming realisation that not only was my daughter rejecting her gender, but also the name we had so lovingly chosen and called her for the past twenty years. I was starting to sink into panic and distress and could hardly look at my child, never mind feel gratitude that at least he was trying to please me by using a name that we had chosen.

I now understand that these confused feelings were of course entirely normal and natural.

Other parents of children, young people and adults who identify as trans, gender variant, gender fluid, gender non-binary or who have gender dysphoria, have expressed all the same emotions about *losing* the person they thought was their child and in particular struggling with the loss of the precious name. Mothers of trans boys have also recognised that they too were devastated when their daughters told them they needed to be boys, because like me they wanted to create a more positive relationship with their daughters than they had had with their own mothers. One told me that the only reason she was surviving was because she had another daughter. A father said that whilst he had adjusted to his daughter becoming a male, it would have been the end of his world if his son had been the one to express gender dysphoria.

Nevertheless, at the time I had huge feelings of guilt as I felt that I should have been more able to accept Jane's news. Throughout Jane's childhood and adolescence I had taught her that transgender people deserved our support and had a right to be who they really are. Talk about hung by my own petard! Never, in my support for trans people had I given a single thought to what impact their changed identity would have on their parents, siblings or extended family. At the time of Nathan's disclosure it was only adult transgender people who had featured in any media coverage. I had not considered that, of course, children and young people's identities are intimately entwined with those of their parents. I had identified as the parent of a daughter and a son and now this was changing. My own identity felt under threat.

Discussing this feeling with other parents I have discovered that some mothers go through all sorts of psychological and emotional processes to ensure they love their child, regardless of his/her (apparent) gender at birth. For instance, I really wanted a girl and got one, so did not have to adjust my feelings towards her in order to bond. Similarly when I thought it would be nice to have a boy and got one, I was thrilled. As they grew up I told them, truthfully, that they were my favourite daughter and favourite son.

I don't care as long as it's healthy

Mothers have told me that when they would have preferred the opposite gender to that of their children, they have overemphasised their pleasure at having a son or a daughter so that the child does not pick up any feelings that their gender is not the preferred one. In one case this resulted in a trans girl's mother continually saying how glad she was she had a son, thereby adding to her anguish about her child coming out as trans. In reality after the baby's birth the mother had tried hard not to let her true preference for a daughter affect her relationship with her apparent baby boy. I am continually aware that the idea that mothers' and fathers' love might be influenced by gender is taboo in our culture. Interestingly, one trans women explained to me that prior to her son's birth – she was at that time his father – she had wished for a daughter so that she could have all the experiences that she had wanted for herself. She quickly managed to readjust her expectations when the baby was born male, but nevertheless this shows that feelings of preference for a particular gender are not the sole preserve of cis-gendered people (people whose sex characteristics and gender match up).

With all these complex and conflicting thoughts and feelings buzzing around our heads Nathan and I went to the hospital with Colin for his surgery. Ian coped as usual by heading off to work.

CHAPTER 2
Sharing the news

Happily Colin's operation went off without incident, but
Ian and I did not feel we wanted to tell him about Jane/
Nathan's revelations of the previous evening until he had
recovered and was out of hospital. This decision to delay
telling Colin until he left hospital meant that the first person
I told after Ian was Claire, my closest friend and work
colleague.

I went straight to work from the hospital and Claire could
immediately see something was wrong. Over coffee she
appeared completely unfazed by my news. A counsellor by
profession, she had worked with transgender adults and did
not appear to be shocked to hear that Jane needed to transition. Her only distress was around what she now realised
was a totally inappropriate birthday gift the previous evening.
She really regretted that Nathan might have felt uncomfortable
opening such an intimate female gift. I asked Claire if she
would tell the other staff for me and she agreed to do so. By
the afternoon she had written a beautiful letter to Ian and
me in which she recognised that we had been through so
much acknowledging, adjusting and adapting to the realities
of our children's various impairments but that this might feel
like an adjustment too far. She told us she would be alongside

us in our grief and sorrow and would do what she could to support us. This immediate and heartfelt response enabled me to believe that our family and friends would indeed be supportive of Nathan and us.

However, in the immediate aftermath of this revelation I had it in my head that Jane had purposefully inveigled her way into the affection of my staff team to take their support away from me. I therefore shocked the team by declaring that they must have nothing more to do with Jane/Nathan as it was 'inappropriate'. This was so unlike me that it is a great indicator of my distress at the time. One staff member, Sharon, talks about how she was particularly upset by my edict as Jane had struck up a friendship with her disabled daughter and had been enjoying visiting her home. She felt that in an instant both she and her daughter, who saw Jane as an older role model, had lost a valued friend.

Ian was affected in different ways during the aftermath and this was both positive and challenging. Not feeling his own identity under threat by Jane becoming Nathan he was not having conflicted feelings to the same extent as I was. He was able to cope with Nathan's distress. This enabled him to write a lovely letter of love and support to Nathan, which he gave him when he arrived at the hospital. Colin now tells us he knew something was going on because he saw his dad hand Jane the letter, but had no clue what it was about.

At one point that first day Nathan was having a lie down on the spare bed in Colin's cubicle, with his back to the door, and a doctor asked 'Is that Colin's brother?' – she had glanced at their camouflage t-shirt, combat trousers and short hair and made this assumption. That was my first exposure to others viewing Nathan as he needed to be and I replied 'Yes', thinking how pleased Nathan would be to have 'passed'. But I felt ambivalent and this would dog me for a number of years – delight that my child was being recognised for who he needed to be, coupled with grief and regret about the loss of my daughter and fear for his future.

As the parent of two disabled children I had been in this position numerous times before – feeling one emotion whilst also holding another opposing position simultaneously and needing to present a face to my child or others which was not how I was feeling inside. It is known as 'cognitive dissonance' and is recognised as an extremely stressful and exhausting mental state. Having gone through it before does not necessarily reduce the impact. In fact I think that having had years of this added to my distress and its cumulative effect made it even harder to live with. After all my years of therapy I am better able to identify what is happening to me, but this doesn't always help. It can also mean I am unable to protect the person who needs me to be inauthentic. If I unwittingly leak my real feelings this simply adds guilt into the mix. Having worked through all this with Nathan, once he was psychologically well enough for me to do so, has really helped me to move on and be authentic around him. This is much healthier for both of us.

What all of this highlights is that at a time when a trans child, young person or adult needs the wholehearted support of their parents and siblings, their family members may also be extremely fragile and least able to respond well.

On the Saturday following Nathan's revelation we agreed that he and I would go shopping for his new clothes and Ian would take on the task of telling Colin and some of our closest friends. This had a poignant familiarity as this is what happened seventeen years before when Colin was born and Ian had to call people to break the news and deal with other people's responses alongside his own shock and grief.

Colin recalls an overwhelming, visceral reaction to his dad telling him the news: He 'freaked out and rushed to the bathroom to vomit'. He describes imagining his sister undergoing a biological, reptilian, transformation whereby she turned from a 'butch lesbian' into a 'rugby playing ogre' of a man with no likeness to the sibling he had grown up with and loved. He also describes his bewilderment, as he recalls Jane talking, like me, from a feminist perspective, and often objecting to some of her dad's comments which she saw as sexist. As Colin himself does not identify as an alpha male, the thought that his sibling would turn into that was understandably distressing. So too was his concern that it would change the dynamic of their relationship.

Colin's response to all his initial feelings was to flee. He packed a bag and left the house in great distress. Ian found him at Waverley Station en route to stay with his Aunty Pat. Ian managed to persuade him to stay in Edinburgh and arranged for an overnight stay closer to home.

Now reflecting on their growing up together Colin recalls not 'seeing' Jane's gender when they were small, but remembers her being protective of him when they were growing up and he saw protectiveness as a feminine trait. They were tactile, expressed loved to each other and shared hugs. He attributed these physical displays of affection to the fact she was female – seeing me as the predominant hugger.

This was reinforced by the fact that he did not see brothers he knew behaving in these ways. On the contrary these fraternal relationships were characterised by 'rough and tumble'. However, later he could see that brothers did often behave in caring ways towards each other.

Colin also recounts not having a problem with Jane's lesbianism. Although he recalls crying when she told him because he had previously made jokes about lesbians and he felt guilty! Despite his initial feelings Colin accepted Nathan's transition quite quickly because it became apparent that gender 'was no big deal' in their relationship. What's more, he did not feel that his sibling changed towards him. All that really changed was Nathan's outward physical presentation.

When questioned about whether he felt his relationship to his sibling had been different to those of other brothers and sisters they had known, Colin replied that in the only family they were close to, they had had similarly 'genderless' relationships. No doubt this was due to the fact that I was drawn to similarly feminist women who were consciously treating their children as equals and not perpetuating gender stereotypes. In retrospect, Colin feels that the relationship between Ian and Jane was not that of a typical father/daughter relationship where there is closeness and affection. He recalls that they were often in conflict and never really got on.

Ian and I are so delighted our two sons are close and that Nathan's transition has not been a barrier to their developing this extremely valuable and mutually supportive relationship.

Friends and family

Colin's need to get away from Nathan that first day, to 'sort out' his feelings was enabled by our close friends, Carol and Errol who gave him a bed for the night. When Ian had arrived at their home to break the news, the first thing they did was to text Nathan and myself messages of love and to say this would not change their relationship with him. This was not only lovely but the reaction I had predicted from friends and colleagues when I had discussed the matter with Ian. When he had first heard of Nathan's coming out as transgender, Ian had gone to a really dark place, imagining strangers daubing hate messages on our doors and the girls in my Guide unit's parents wanting to withdraw their daughters. In short they would equate transgender with paedophilia. He can now see that his fears were due to the fact that the social context eleven years ago was far less supportive of trans people and the rhetoric in much of the media at the time was deeply homo and trans phobic. Again this was his cognitive dissonance: he was able to support Nathan whilst at the same fearing the stigma and backlash we might all experience.

Whether naive or just in denial, I did not have these fears myself and, when considering who to tell, could not imagine any of our family or friends having an issue with it. I was wrong. No one was overt in saying they felt uncomfortable with the news, but we have lost some people from our lives. Some of them were more than likely uncomfortable either as a result of their faith or due to trans or homophobia.

Our friend Carol remembers being initially shocked, but then thinking that Jane had been experimenting in her dress and presentation over her teenage years, trying to find herself and that now she had realised who she needed to be. Carol feels that her personality didn't change. He was the 'same person' with the same sense of humour and funny express-ions.

I was in great distress, however, telling my sister Pat about Nathan as I knew she felt very close to Jane. I was aware it would be painful for her personally as well as seeing me in distress. At the time she was very supportive, saying that nothing would change how she and my brother-in-law felt about Nathan. She now describes feeling shocked. She is also aware that she felt a sense of loss at the time and describes getting out all of her photographs of Jane's school holiday visits. She remembers her as a pretty child with lovely blonde hair and high intelligence. She noticed Jane's style changing in her early teens as she opted for clothes that Pat describes as 'alternative, not neat and tidy girl clothing – more masculine'. She thought this was simply about Jane finding out who she was and exploring her identity. Pat liked Jane's long-term lesbian partner and remembers thinking she was happy as a lesbian woman.

Her late husband Bill was very close to Jane but nonetheless just accepted Nathan as he was. Nathan was concerned that Bill might struggle with his transition but he didn't express any negativity. Pat says his only concern that was that the surgery was too soon. Otherwise Bill just worried that he would make a mistake and call Nathan, Jane. Pat also describes watching my grief and shock as 'horrendous'. She recounts feeling very worried about me and my need to get away from Nathan in those early days. But she understood this as a need for me to gather my thoughts and she expresses admiration at the way I then 'got on with it'. She also appreciated how supportive I was of him thereafter.

The rest of our siblings and extended family took the news with equanimity and if they felt any discomfort they did not express that openly to us. This was very helpful. My sister's daughter, Carole, and her two children were particularly accepting and welcoming of Nathan.

I was not close to my brother, who had left home to join the navy when I was 4, but he and my sister-in-law expressed support by sending their Christmas card a few months later to 'Ian, Shirley and the boys' which was a subtle way of showing acceptance. Their lovely daughters, Nathan's cousins, have also always been accepting, which has been very comforting for me. The latest, delightful, addition to the family is Colin's fiancé, Brittany. They have a long distance relationship as she lives in New York. When asked how she felt that her fiancé had a transgender brother, she simply said she was curious to learn more. Although she was comfortable with the idea Brittany says that prior to meeting Nathan she felt more nervous, and asked herself how she should act appropriately. Quite rightly she decided to just be herself and treat Nathan 'like anyone else'.

To let the rest of our wider friendship circles know about Nathan we decided, with his agreement, to write a letter in which we stated that he needed to be a man, that we were supporting him and that we would welcome their support at this difficult time. We also asked them to tell any mutual friends or acquaintances so that I would not have to go through people asking me how 'my beautiful daughter' was. We sent a second letter to all the professionals who were involved in Nathan's and Colin's life as a result of their impairments. Once again we asked people to spread the word, as my position at SNIP meant I came into contact with so many people in my professional capacity. My children had been part of my professional life all the time they were growing up, as I used our experiences as a family to illustrate training sessions, lectures and speeches.

Ironically, although people expressed support, they did not pass on the news and in some cases made a point of telling me 'they hadn't told anybody', thereby reinforcing our feelings that this was a stigmatising event we were living through. This increased our feelings of isolation.

Nathan, however, saw the issue differently. He thinks it may be due to Scottish middle class reserve and discomfort around 'gossiping' rather than due to the subject matter itself.

But feelings of isolation did accompany those first few days. Just as when Colin was born, it felt like a living nightmare where I kept thinking I would wake up and it would not be true. As with a bereavement, we felt like keeping the curtains closed and hunkering down to wait for the funeral. But there was no funeral, no flowers, no understanding from other people who had been through this grief. Just us trying to make sense of something that seemed senseless. Leading up to Nathan's 'butch' presentation we had had a teenage lesbian daughter who loved nothing more that piling on the sparkly pink and purple eye-shadow and had enough nail varnish to keep the local chemists in business. This was the daughter who shared dressing rooms with me, and with whom I shared intimate thoughts and feelings that I would not have shared with a teenage son. Trying to get our heads around every new dawning of what we thought was 'true' being presented back to us as something that had been unbearable for our child was incredibly challenging. Nathan explains that he also struggled to understand what he was feeling, since he felt male whilst at the same time finding applying the make-up and nail varnish totally appealing.

A trans man who transitioned at the same age as Nathan once explained to me that what he and possibly other trans people are doing is asking to be viewed 'through a different lens'. However, in the process they do not necessarily realise (or need to deny for their own well-being) that when they edit their own history they are editing other family members' history as well, thereby forgetting that those family members also need to tell their stories – stories from which the trans person is often trying to distance themselves. This is because socially, at the time he and Nathan were transitioning, the trans person needed to 'prove' themselves as legitimately the opposite gender from that which was apparent at birth. He describes not knowing what history to retain and which to delete. He also expresses relief at keeping his childhood photographs, a feeling echoed by parents I have spoken to, when their own child wanted them destroyed.

With hindsight I now understand that it must have been horrendous for Jane that I was very open about puberty and wanted to provide her with the tools to enter womanhood without fear. I was therefore delighted to take her for her first bra, explain all about periods and so on, but to my bemusement she seemed not to welcome this, whereas when I was given this information I responded with excitement. I put this down to us being different personalities and thought she was simply embarrassed by my enthusiasm for everything menstrual! I don't recall checking out with her what was going on at the time, but can now imagine how excruciating this must have been for her.

Developing sexuality

When Jane was 15 I pulled up to the school gate to take her to an orchestra and saw her looking so tenderly at her best friend and giving her a kiss on her lips. It was then that I understood that they were in an intimate relationship. When she came out to me a few weeks later I was initially fine. She asked me to break the news to Ian which I did. He was also unfazed at the fact that she was now identifying as lesbian. And then to my shame and guilt, two weeks later I was grief-stricken because all my expectations of helping my daughter navigate relationships with men had now been taken away. I also thought that it might mean that there would be no opportunity for me to pass on all my wisdom about being a mother. It felt that yet another door was closing on what I thought I was able to bring to parenting my precious daughter – my 'mini-me'.

It never occurred to me then that I was trying to re-parent myself. I now realise that as my own mother developed a severe mental illness when I was ten my own experience of being mothered had been compromised. This made me determined to give my own daughter a 'perfect mothering' experience. Psychoanalysts, like Susie Orbach, confirm that the mother-daughter relationship can be very challenging, with mothers encouraging their daughters to be independent long before they take the same steps with their sons. This can result in the 'incomplete' mothering of girls which leads them in turn to struggle to mother their own daughters. This unconscious drive to push Jane away when she was young, coupled with my own neediness, meant I did what my mum had done to me. In other words, I looked to my teenage daughter for emotional support, particularly when she and her brother were growing up and my husband was emotionally absent due to his grief and loss around Colin's impairments and his difficulties at work.

Looking back I can see that Jane's aggression towards Ian may have resulted from her acting out the role of oldest son thereby competing with the father for the affection of the mother. Jane had always supported me when I was having a feminist rant about men in general and her dad in particular but now all that support that I had taken as female solidarity was taking on a whole new meaning. I suddenly had to confront my own understanding of gender, identity and mothering role.

Consequently, in the days following Nathan's revelation I flip-flopped from compassion to shame, from grief to anger. I could not respond to what felt like opposing requests from Nathan – to love him as much as I had before his coming out, but to accept that he was not the daughter I thought he was.

Before hormone treatment Nathan looked far younger dressed as a male than he had as a woman. This meant that Ian and I felt like a 20 year old 'boy' had turned up on our doorstep and declared he was our long-lost son. It may sound trivial but Nathan didn't smell the same as Jane. This felt like another huge loss. We had joked as a family that I could pick them all out blindfolded as I was so sensitive to their smell. This is common in the animal kingdom and explains why mothers can reject their young if humans handle them. Nathan did not look, smell or sound like my child. Intellectually I knew he was still my offspring but at a deeply human-animal level I did not feel it. This triggered terrible nightmares in which my daughter was lost and calling for me. I could not get to her and I would wake up with the pillow soaked with tears.

By the third or fourth day after Jane became Nathan I followed Colin's suit and had to get away from Nathan to get space to grieve. Once again Carol and Errol provided that haven. I cried and cried until my head throbbed, my throat was raw and my eyes all but disappeared.

I understand now I had to start thinking of Jane and Nathan as two separate people. I had to do this so that I could accept Nathan's new presentation and to start using his chosen name and appropriate pronouns which at that time were 'he' and 'him'. In those days I was in the privileged position of using taxis fairly regularly in the course of my work. I used every journey as an opportunity to talk about my two sons, Nathan and Colin. Sitting behind the driver without making eye contact helped me to rehearse this narrative until it became normalised and I started to feel it was true. One mother at the TransParenTsees Support group also did this describing it as 'faking it until you make it'. However, this splitting my child up into two personas allowed me to keep feeling angry with Nathan for taking Jane away from me. This did not help our relationship and added to his distress.

Inevitably, as Nathan grew impatient with me not being able

to be around him and make the adjustments he needed quickly enough we started to argue. In one exchange he berated me for treating gender as so important. He now can see that he had had a number of years to understand and accept what was happening to him, whereas I had only a few days. He came to see that it was too much for me to immediately acknowledge, adjust and adapt to this new reality. However, he needed to know that I was not going to reject him.

In the immediate aftermath of his disclosure I had reassured him of my continued love and support but my subsequent behaviour was very distressing for him. I felt guilty for this but my overwhelming grief and feelings of loss – both around this traumatic event and the triggering of all my previous losses – meant I could not immediately put my feelings aside.

I also adopted coping mechanisms that were potentially damaging. I stopped eating and sure enough I lost over a stone in the first few weeks. My friend Claire eventually told me she would no longer go for meals with me, one of our favourite things to do, if I was just going to push the food round the plate! That brought me up sharp and although I was angry with her at the time, I consciously put more food in my mouth and gradually my appetite improved. Wine became a comfort. Ian and I had always enjoyed a couple of glasses together at the weekend but over the years, when I was often working away from home, this had extended to a couple of weekdays as well. Under the stress of Nathan's disclosure we started opening a bottle of wine every night to take the edge off our pain. The alcohol provided a welcome anaesthetic but since it is also a depressant it made our mood even worse. As well as the obvious dangers of alcoholism and other health issues we were not helping our mood by using alcohol to cope.

I was already accessing counselling around Colin's disability. Prior to Nathan coming out as trans I was gutted when this counsellor started voicing opinions about his decisions, saying it 'was all too fast for him to know he needed to be a man'. I stopped seeing her, after fleeing her house in distress. I knew that I would have to start all over again with someone new. Luckily, as well as my close female friends and staff team, at work I had a fantastically supportive practice supervisor, Rachel, and she provided an invaluable level of support whilst I sought a new therapist.

At the same time as we were struggling with all this, Ian and I were also going to work full-time and caring for Colin who, in preparation for living independently from us, had personal assistants who would come to the house and feed him during the day. Every night the district nurse would come and set up his overnight feeding tube. Colin had just left college and was leaving for university in September, but his 18th birthday, just two weeks after Nathan's memorable 20th passed in a blur. So too did our wedding anniversary a couple of days previously, where I managed to drink so much bubbly that at one point I sat down on the pavement on the way home and refused to get up. Thankfully, I had exceptionally loyal and supportive staff and employers during this time, who helped me develop less damaging ways of coping.

One thing they were all adamant about was that I must not destroy any family photographs. The distress I was feeling meant I could not look at any pictures of Jane. I felt as though nothing I thought I knew was true any more and the pain of looking at photographs of her was too much to bear. Claire offered to take them from me and store them to avoid me doing anything rash, but I was able to take heed of her suggestion and we put them away in a cupboard. One of my favourites was of Jane in her Guide uniform, me in my Guider's uniform and Colin dressed for Cubs. It had had pride of place in our family home and was now on the wall in the flat we had downsized to, just a few months before Nathan's news.

At the time I shared an office with Carrie Upton, the wonderful hospital chaplain at the Royal Hospital for Sick Children Edinburgh, where SNIP was based. She encouraged me to follow the example of bereaved parents and take this picture and other precious things of Jane's and make a keepsake box. It was absolutely heartbreaking for me to put hair clips, skating badges, ribbons, and other items into what had been her make-up box. A box I had bought so proudly for her and she had revelled in using. My deprived working-class background had led me to buy her a lot of cheap, sentimental gifts over the previous few years; one was a sign that said 'A daughter is a little girl who grows up to be a friend'. Another was a keepsake book for daughters with tips from mothers. All the things I had wished a mum had given to me I had lavished on my daughter and I placed them all carefully into the box, finishing off with a letter of farewell. I wept as I wrote it. This was another of Carrie's suggestions.

In the years since, as I have taken out the letter and reread it and touched the items and photographs, I have been so grateful to her. These mementoes have given validity to my understanding of those years before Jane became who she needed to be. It took me a while to be able to revisit the box, but I am so glad I put it together because it now provides me with the type of comfort visiting a grave gives.

CHAPTER 3
Coping with transition

In the midst of all of this trauma and Colin's imminent departure to Loughborough we were also trying to access support for Nathan. He told us he had been receiving fantastic emotional support from LGBT Youth Scotland over the past five years and that he felt it was now time for him to access medical interventions for his gender dysphoria.

I took him to our wonderful GP Barry Parker, who had seen us through many of the children's medical emergencies He was lovely and referred Nathan to Dr Lyndsey Myskow, who at that time was the only psychiatrist in Scotland specialising in gender identity issues.

Ian says it was this visit, to which he accompanied Nathan, that helped him to understand what was going on for Nathan. His need to become male was borne out by Dr Myskow's assessment. Her certainty that Nathan did indeed have gender dysphoria dispelled any worries Ian might have had as to whether Nathan was making the right decision pursuing hormone treatment and surgery so that his body and brain would be in harmony. However, it quickly became clear that unless we were prepared to wait two years, this surgery would not be available on the NHS.

Another of my established coping mechanisms, cultivated over the twenty years of seeking information about Colin and Nathan's various illnesses and impairments as well as in my professional role in doing the same for very many families, was to research everything known about gender dysphoria and its treatment. I was therefore dismayed, but not surprised, to hear that Nathan would be put through the ignominy (as we then saw it) of having to 'pass' as male for a year before being prescribed hormones. As he could prove to Dr Myskow that he had been doing so prior to his return home, this was slightly shortened, but his distress at being 'out' and not immediately able to progress his transition was evident.

When we asked about psychological support for Nathan during his transition, again the response was either a lengthy wait on the NHS or we could 'choose' to go private. As Nathan had been suicidal, the idea that this was a choice felt offensive and inappropriate. Luckily we *were* in a position to pay for counselling and we accessed this via the private medical practice from which Dr Myskow worked. At that time the NHS Child & Adolescent Mental Health Service was operating under straitened circumstances and this has only become worse. What the outcome would have been for Nathan had we been unable to pay doesn't bear thinking about.

My relationship with Nathan was still highly compromised. As I was still struggling to get past my grief we decided that in order to aid my recovery and be once more the mum he needed, we must live apart. We supported him to apply for social housing which, given his disability and mental health issues, he was eligible for. Ian went to visit flats with him. The first one they viewed was deeply depressing and totally inappropriate for someone as vulnerable as Nathan, but the second at The Shore in Leith was just perfect and our gratitude to the Port of Leith Housing Association knows no bounds. It was just the right size and in a fantastic location. We would not have chosen the set of circumstances that led to him moving there, but it provided us each with the space we needed to adjust to the changes and renegotiate our relationship.

For Nathan's first Christmas as a man, we went out for lunch with Claire and her family and he looked so young and smart in his suit. I was so anxious that someone would use the wrong pronoun but it all went really well. Nonetheless it felt surreal to me as I embraced his new presentation. I tried to make some amends for my difficulties in coming to terms with his transition by giving him a bundle of toys that he 'missed out' on when he was young. They included a wooden pull-along train and a Bob the Builder tool kit! He was really pleased at this acknowledgement and thereafter our relationship started to improve.

Nathan still struggled with the idea that he had to wait for two years to have his breasts removed. I was struggling to live in the home with a bedroom that I had created for my daughter. So we decided to downsize again to a cheaper property. This killed several birds with one stone – providing the fresh start I needed as well as the funding for Nathan's surgery.

Before we put the house on the market Nathan was badly beaten up. I was at work one January morning when I got the call from Ian to say Nathan had rung from an ambulance taking him to Edinburgh's Royal Infirmary. He and his friend had been sitting on a bench in Princes Street Gardens taking photographs of the castle. Nathan had noticed a group of young men messing about at the fountain and felt a little vulnerable. However, while they were still seated and before they had the chance to move away a couple of the youths ran over and started punching Nathan in the face. He managed to shout at them and believes his feminine sounding voice was what stopped them from inflicting even more damage. Bloodied and bruised Nathan looked around for someone to help them and his friend dialled 999. People passed but did not stop. Only a couple of female tourists, seeing Nathan's injuries, finally came and assisted.

I put the phone down in the office and burst into tears as I waited for Ian to arrive in the car. We travelled to the hospital in traumatised numbness, not knowing how seriously injured our darling son was. Although he was in a head and neck brace when we arrived, Nathan was beaming from ear to ear as he told us he had finally entered manhood – he had been beaten up! What's more, he told us that the police, paramedics and hospital staff were very understanding, treating him with utmost respect and telling them he didn't have to undress for the x-ray. The young people were caught and their parents expressed great remorse about the attack. Nathan and the police thought that the young men had assumed that since a quite effeminate young man was with his male friend they thought they were a couple. The attack was therefore considered a homophobic hate crime. Due to the age of the young men involved however the police decided not to take the case further.

In true Nathan fashion he was sorry for the plight of the

offenders. He wondered how difficult their lives must have been for them to feel the need to assault a total stranger.

Nathan's attack left us feeling vulnerable but we soon rallied. Shortly after, despite feeling very anxious about the many changes that were about to happen to his body, Nathan began his treatment with male hormones. This anxiety was no doubt heightened by the type of impairments I outlined earlier which makes change particularly challenging for him. Nonetheless soon he did seem decidedly more male, with legs hairier than his dad's and a deepening voice.

We then started to investigate his options for surgery. He had put on hold his application to university to the autumn, so that he could arrive there in his new gender and with his new chest.

A new life, a new love

Before Jane went down south to work at Colin's former school she had completed an HNC in Acting and Performance at Edinburgh's Telford College. Her audition piece had been a monologue for a girl where she talked about her dad wishing she were a boy! I remember going to see the end-of-course performance of Medea and for once not seeing Jane's different style of hair as quirky but as odd. She did not move like any of the other young women, who looked glamorous with their long blonde hair and feminine movements, but I simply put it down to her arthritis. Naturally, feeling male, it had been so disappointing for her to have to play female roles, so once Nathan was back in Edinburgh during his transition, a couple of months before he was due to have his surgery, he joined a community play being put on by Theatre Workshop called 'Black Sun over Genoa'. The play describes the death of a protester at the hands of the police at the G8 summit in Genoa, a few years previously. It was put on to coincide with the G8 summit being held that year in Gleneagles. A young man called Robert Softley was in the audience one night. He was immediately drawn to the handsome actor – Nathan-playing a wheelchair-using character. Robert found out that Nathan was going to Gleneagles to protest against the summit the following day and swiftly arranged to do likewise! In conversation they discovered they had mutual friends and interests in common. The following week they had their first date and after their second date Nathan invited Robert back to his flat, because he had something he needed to tell him.

Robert recounts that he had no suspicions that Nathan was anything other than cis-male – a person whose gender identity matches their sex characteristics. He felt nervous about hearing what Nathan felt he needed to tell him. He was surprised and hadn't been expecting this disclosure. Robert recalls having to think through what being the boyfriend of a trans man meant for his own identity. Fortunately he had already worked through his own sexuality and was comfortable with the idea that things did not have to 'fit into black and white'. He found Nathan 'hugely attractive' and, being empathetic himself, he didn't want him to suffer rejection. He also understood the risk Nathan had taken in telling him.

As soon as Nathan told me about Robert I knew that we had met many times before. Robert has cerebral palsy and is a wheelchair user and we had sat on various disability-related committees and working groups. A bright, confident young man with a beautiful face and fantastic smile, he was in my view an ideal role model for Colin.

Within weeks Nathan brought Robert to the flat to introduce us and have dinner. Although Nathan had told Rob that we had met, he couldn't place me from Nathan's description. As I stood at the door and he came down the path towards me his face was a picture as he said 'I don't believe it – it's you!'

Within weeks they were inseparable and when the time came to travel to London for the operation, Nathan announced Robert was coming too. Ian and I travelled to London for the surgery a week before we were due to move to our new home.

Nathan was so excited to be getting his new chest that he was in good spirits as the surgeon explained the procedure on the morning of the operation. I reassured him all would be fine and that this was the start of the rest of his life. Yet at the same time I felt horrified that my child's perfect breasts were about to be removed. Many of the patients in adjoining rooms in the private hospital were undergoing cosmetic procedures. I saw men coming to visit and I suspected that they were 'encouraging' their partners to undergo facelifts and breast enlargements. I was so torn between feelings of distaste and distress that these perfectly attractive women felt the need to do this to themselves and gratitude that operating on them had given Nathan's surgeon the skills required for his operation.

Following the operation Robert sat the whole night at Nathan's bedside. That's what you call love.

Waiting for Nathan to come out of his follow-up appointment at the surgeon's Harley Street clinic a few days later was one of the most nerve-racking of my life. I so hoped that he would be pleased with the result. He had been shown pictures of what 'normal' male chests look like to help him understand that there is not one 'right' chest and I just hoped that his new one was going to be to his liking.

His beaming smile as he came back into the waiting room said it all and the £5,000 we had spent now meant nothing. I was so relieved and hopeful that things would now settle down again. After all Nathan was now the man he needed to be, without the breasts that had caused him so much grief.

My crisis

Thanks to my wonderful employers at SNIP I was able to take a couple of months off work to be available for him during and after the surgery and to recover from what I expected to be a traumatic experience for us both. I really used the time well, doing a great deal of howling (much to the discomfort of our downstairs neighbour) and accessing therapy.

Looking back I can see that at the time I was going through an existential crisis. If my daughter wasn't my daughter then what else wasn't true? I felt as though I could trust nothing and started to doubt whether anything I had understood about my relationship with her had been real.

I also felt completely disorientated as most of my usual self-soothing strategies were linked to my family: if I couldn't get to sleep then I would remember holidays we had had or funny things the children had said. Now every image of Jane brought pain. I could not think back to the past nor feel any hope for the future. Like someone with memory problems, I was locked in the here and now. This was excruciatingly painful.

So it is hardly surprising that I started to feel that the only escape was death and so had occasional suicidal thoughts. Sometimes I found it a comfort to know that I could stop this pain. However, I knew that this course of action would be so much more painful for those around me. I didn't want to alarm them so I said nothing. Other times I felt so frightened by my thoughts that I made a point of sharing my feelings with my therapist so that I didn't act on them.

Apart from my therapist, I didn't want to contact other parents of transgender children to get support as I felt I had 'been there and done that' when I was dealing with Nathan's and Colin's impairments. I also realised that since I had run a helpline for many years I would have high expectations from anyone offering support. So I was reluctant to contact the limited organisations that were available at that time.

Eventually I felt that I had to speak to another mother who was going through what I was experiencing. I wanted to hear that what I was going through was natural, normal and was shared by others. Unfortunately the mum I spoke to on the phone was so far down the line of acknowledging, adjusting and adapting to her trans son's transition that she was incapable of empathising with my distress. She also said that she had never really bothered about having a daughter, that she had always seemed masculine and so it was not a problem for her as a mother. I felt gutted. To not be heard and to get the impression that what I was going through was somehow odd, when I was feeling so fragile and vulnerable, was incredibly distressing. I regret now, that it deterred me from contacting anyone else in the transparenting community to discuss the issue.

It was the love from Ian, Nathan and Colin that helped me get through. So too did the letter from my friend Claire which said I would survive this and that she would be there for me. The support of family and other brilliant friends also helped me keep going.

Adjustments

As I grappled with my own feeling of loss I was managing to take comfort in Nathan's happiness. Sadly this soon changed. Nathan's positive response to his new chest was short-lived. Within a couple of years his mood darkened once again and his eating disorder returned with a vengeance. His mental health deteriorated and he entered a downward spiral of self-harming, anorexia and suicidal thoughts. Nathan got an appointment at the psychiatric hospital but they said they had nothing to offer him, that there was a waiting list of around nine months for an outpatient appointment and that as Nathan's self-harming was providing him with an outlet for his distress, under the circumstances this was the least worst option as a coping strategy. It is well recognised that self harming by cutting is an emotional release which is preferabe to suicide but at the time I felt shocked by this response. They thought that all his distress was due to his gender identity issues and that as we had accessed private medical support in the past we could afford to continue to do so. They did not check with us if this was the case.

My fear was that even if we could afford to buy therapy for Nathan, it might not be the right or best treatment for him. It felt like we were in some warped game of pass the parcel, where everyone in general mental health services kept saying we needed to speak to the specialists but they in turn told us to go to the generalists. . . It also felt that because we had made a decision in desperation, to go private, this was now acting against us and that NHS staff in mental health services felt we were no longer eligible for their care.

The nine months that followed were terrible: Nathan made a number of serious attempts to kill himself. We all lived with dreadful fear and anxiety. We were effectively on 24-hour suicide watch, which Nathan found so difficult yet we couldn't trust him to be alone. When Rob was away I went to their home or Nathan moved in with us.

Looking back, Nathan can see that although he was adamant that he needed breast surgery, the speed he accessed it meant that he was overwhelmed by his feelings and that it might have been better if things had moved at a slower pace. He realised that it was only after the surgery that he fully grasped the enormity of what he had been through. Even though he was seeing a therapist at the time he did not work through his feelings adequately which is why his mental health suffered in the year following surgery. He also explains that he did not want to die: He just wanted his pain and anguish to end and death seemed to be the only way this would happen.

However, we cannot know whether slowing the pace would have produced a different outcome, since as has been clear from his early life there are so many other factors that had the potential to undermine his mental health. Nonetheless knowing what he knows now, Nathan feels he might not have taken the hormones and just had the breast surgery instead, since he does not enjoy having facial hair.

In addition to the wonderful love and support given to him by Robert, a beacon of light within the darkness of Nathan's suicidal time was his therapist from the mental health charity Penumbra. Nathan accessed this therapy during the wait for the psychiatric hospital appointment. Without her incredibly skilled input I doubt Nathan would have survived.

Finally, following three suicide attempts he got the treatment he needed. On release from the hospital a community psychiatric nurse told Ian and myself to 'take him home but there is nothing you can do to stop him killing himself if he is determined.' Thankfully he didn't and finally began his treatment at the Eating Disorders Unit, in the Cullen Centre at the Royal Edinburgh Hospital. He had promised to attend an eating disorders group and a one-to-one session of Dialectical Behavioural Therapy for a year. We cannot thank his therapist enough for her work with him. By the end of the year he was eating better and feeling better about himself. We were delighted when he and Rob announced their engagement and planned a civil partnership.

They decided that rather than make up a list of presents, they would invite guests to make a donation to the Cullen Centre. Nathan asked what would be useful and his therapist said some books for parents. They finally handed over £1,500 to the centre, which they spent on the books and a coffee machine for parents in the waiting room.

Our joy around Nathan and Rob's civil partnership was, understandably, tinged with some worry about whether our old expectations of Ian walking his daughter down the aisle and my dreams of being the 'mother of the bride', would affect our enjoyment of making the plans and the event itself.

We need not have fretted. It was a wonderful day that neither Ian nor I could have imagined being able to attend just a few years earlier.

Following his therapy and civil partnership ceremony, Nathan felt he could start to look forward. He had already completed some incredibly important milestones such as having his birth certificate and passport changed to reflect his new gender identity. He applied successfully to undertake a law degree at Napier University and again, with hard work and the right support did incredibly well, finishing with a first class honours degree. He then moved to Edinburgh University, where he completed his Diploma in Legal Practice. No one could have been prouder than Ian, Colin, Robert and I as we attended each of these graduation ceremonies. Given what Nathan had been through and continued to have to deal with, his outstanding success was beyond our wildest hopes and dreams.

On finishing his diploma, Nathan was delighted to go to work for the Equality Network. His exact title was the Transgender Policy Officer for the Scottish Transgender Alliance. Nathan believes using one's talents, skills and own lived experience to raise awareness and support others in a similar predicament can help individuals make sense of and add to the meaning of their own lives. Ian, Colin and I couldn't agree more. For two years he championed and worked with the Scottish Government on the Same Sex Marriage Bill and Act. We were so proud when the legislation changed to enable same sex couples to get married knowing that Nathan had helped make this happen. In August 2015 Nathan started a two-year traineeship in the public sector to complete his legal training to become a solicitor.

Another transition

Over the past few years Nathan's gender identity has developed and he has come to consider himself to be 'non-binary'. This recognises that he has both masculine and feminine parts of his gender. Quite simply it means that Nathan doesn't feel that the terms male or female adequately describe who he is. As a consequence, Nathan now prefers the gender neutral pronoun 'they' as opposed to 'he' or 'she' to describe himself – or themselves as Nathan prefers. Using these pronouns is something we have all found a challenge to get right but it's important that we show our respect for Nathan's identity in this way. I shall do so in the pages that follow.

CHAPTER 5
Recovery

As I write this book, my thoughts wander to a time when I am sitting on a beach in Majorca. Jane is 11. I can feel the sun on my face, the sand is tickling my feet and the sound of the waves on the shore lulls me to sleep. Suddenly I hear her shouting 'Mum, Mum look I'm doing cartwheels'. And I picture her, with her shoulder length blonde hair and her lovely little athletic body in her swimming costume. And then I over-write it with an image I have created of Nathan, with his blonde hair and swimming trunks. And it doesn't hurt. It is all real. She was her and him and they.

Although I would never have chosen for my child to have gone through this experience, I can be comforted again by reliving their childhood and thinking ahead to when they are a fantastic lawyer who will help to change the world.

So what, apart from the passage of time, has brought me to this place of mental and physical well-being? When Nathan's mental health was deteriorating it all became too much for me and I brought forward my plan to leave my job at SNIP. This would give me some space to look after myself and be more available to Nathan. I remember sitting in my counsellor's room discussing how I needed to separate myself more from my children, as constantly over-empathising with their distress was affecting my own mental health. To continue to support them I needed to be well. My counsellor asked me to imagine taking up a new interest and introducing myself to a new group of people without using the words 'Parent of two disabled sons, one of whom is transgender'. I sat with tears pouring down my face for 45 minutes unable to introduce myself without those words. It was a turning point for me.

My transformation

First I went to the doctor to talk about my drinking. This had become habitual and I was averaging 35 units of alcohol per week. This is classed as heavy drinking. Dr Barry Parker was as lovely as ever and asked me if I could stop if I wanted? I replied that I felt I could and he took some blood to see if I had sustained any liver damage. I feel so lucky that I was both able to cut my intake to below recommended levels and that my blood test was normal. I felt this was a second chance and it encouraged me to look at the rest of my health. I had promised myself I would be 'fit in my fifties' and here I was at 52, far from it.

Support for my increased fitness came from an unexpected source. I was going to London to attend a life-coaching course, part of my new 'portfolio career' made up of public appointments, training and consultancy. My fellow students used the issue of my fitness to practise their developing skills on me. They helped me to create a plan for getting fit. I followed it to the letter and was delighted to send out an email to the group when I had run my first 5k race.

For the first few years I ran purely for myself, using the space to meditate or think through any problems I was dealing with. Then a friend suggested I run a half-marathon with her and I gained sponsorship to raise money for Pancreatic Cancer Research. I was keen on this charity as my sister's husband had sadly died that year of this illness only seven weeks after his diagnosis. I completed the race in 2 hours, 41 minutes and felt triumphant. I have gone on to run a further two half-marathons and various other distances, thoroughly enjoying the discipline of the training and the tremendous feeling of well-being that comes from physical activity out in the fresh air. Ian was inspired by my example and three years ago started going to the gym regularly, as well as cycling and playing golf.

In addition, after reading a coaching book which reported that when women go back to hobbies they had enjoyed as girls they often felt invigorated, I revisited my teenage love of playing a brass instrument. I started to play the trumpet. Once I had mastered reading the music and which valves to press for which note, I joined a local community wind-band. I introduced myself as 'Shirley who used to play a bugle and enjoys running and going to the theatre.' It was weeks before I mentioned either son to the group.

Finally, I started to feel that Person Centred Counselling had become less useful to me than it had before and if anything seemed to be adding to my distress. I wondered if it was like opening an old wound and not letting it heal. I therefore went on the British Association of Counselling and Psychotherapy website and researched alternative approaches. During my time at SNIP, Claire and I had identified that much of my distress seemed to be linked to the traumatic incidents I had endured such as my children's repeated emergency admissions to hospital and that these events had triggered feelings about previous traumas. I found a fantastic Post Traumatic Stress Disorder therapist, Diane, and she worked with me to help me to stop ignoring my body and recognise what it was doing. I found that by adjusting my body I could change how I felt about things including my own emotions. Armed too with Mindfulness and Compassionate Mind Training, I have achieved a level of peace and contentment I once thought was forever out of reach. I also overcame my phobia of heights by using Cognitive Behavioural Therapy and now really enjoy hill-walking with Ian, which is another joy.

To say that Ian, Nathan and Colin are proud of me for turning my life round in this way is an understatement. When they bought me my very own trumpet for Christmas a few years ago I was moved to tears. For someone from my poor background, to own my own musical instrument is something magical.

For myself I am absolutely clear that my recovery was a team effort and that my ability to access love and support from a wide range of people is what enabled me to survive my life challenges. Wonderful friends like Les and Diana lent me their homes to weep. Therapists supported me when I needed to unpick what I was feeling. Friends allowed me to ramble on over copious bottles of wine. Ian stayed alongside me while I travelled my own journey of discovery. I feel grateful to all of them. To Nathan and Colin I want to convey my deepest respect. They make me humble when they deal with everything that life throws at them with humour and grace.

I thought I would never arrive here. I thought I would grieve forever, because it all felt too huge to lose my darling daughter. But of course she was never truly lost. The essence of her was here all the time in the person of my fantastic son, Nathan.

Nathan has been so graceful in their forgiveness of Ian and myself in our not-so-great parenting moments. They have focussed instead on all the good times and the closeness we now all have as a family. Nathan and Ian regularly go for lunch together, just as Ian dreamed of doing with Jane. They enjoy each other's company immensely. Nathan and Colin genuinely love spending time with us and have fantastic relationships with each of us and each other. I am both happy and content.

Furthermore I now understand that people are just people. Some men are interested in other people and have nurturing personalities and some don't. Some women, like my sister, are more interested in sport than relationships. The power of the stereotypes I have internalised is fading but not yet dead. I can still be guilty of assuming that someone will behave in certain ways because of the gender attributed to them at birth. I wish I was more important to my sister than her football team and I know I would be far less bothered if she were a brother!

Within our family, members still make statements assuming future generations will be cis gendered and heterosexual, whilst also embracing Nathan, Rob and me in all our trans, bisexual and queer glory! And how can I blame them? We will always be in a minority. Life in the mainstream is infinitely easier and I understand my passing as straight has smoothed my passage through life in a way that has been denied to my L,G,B,T, Q,I contemporaries.

As a late discoverer of my true sexuality I am ever mindful of not appropriating a space I have not contributed to during the struggle this far for equality. I do not claim to know what life is really like, as trans or disabled, only as a parent. I don't assume I know anything about anyone I meet for the first time now. I ask curious, open questions that do not assume that the person is cis-gendered, heterosexual or non-disabled. I continue to learn every day.

CHAPTER 6
Useful perspectives

Understanding gender

Much of the distress experienced by many trans people and their families would be alleviated if, as a society, we had a much more comprehensive understanding of gender. We continue to make assumptions and place expectations on how people should identify and express their gender. This is based on the sex they were assigned when they were born. This simply fails to recognise the wonderful variety of gender identities and expressions that exist.

I believe that at a superficial level these stereotypes negatively affect all society, limiting the choices people think are available to them. We only need to look at the proportion of female engineers, for example, to understand that many women see certain careers as being for men only. But the effect Western societies' traditional understanding of sex and gender has on trans people is at a much deeper level. At present children are seen and treated in a particular way as a result of the decision that was made about their gender when they were born. But this can be at odds with how they feel about themselves. It can be crushing to learn that society sees a person's assigned sex as an immutable fact. Growing up as a gender variant young person would be so much easier if children could explore their gender through clothes, and toys and play and decide for themselves, when they are ready, how they wanted to identify. This decision would similarly be accompanied by a great deal less angst if they felt confident that it would be ok for their gender identity to change throughout the course of their lives.

Opponents of trans rights often argue by saying 'when I was a girl I liked to climb trees and play with boys but it didn't mean I had to become a man when I grew up'. This reasoning suggests that it is gender stereotypes and the limitations these put on an individual's freedom to behave in typically gendered ways that compel people to transition. But this is a fundamental, and sometimes wilful, misinterpretation of what it is to find your gender identity at odds with your assigned sex. Yes, plenty of people have interests or express themselves in ways that are not typically expected of people of their gender. But that doesn't mean they are trans or feel themselves to be so. It is trans people's own understanding of their gender, how they feel about themselves and their bodies, and how they want their gender to be seen and understood by others, that causes them to transition.

Put most simply, someone who was assigned female at birth, who identifies as a woman and who enjoys football would say 'the fact that I enjoy football doesn't make me any less of a woman,' whereas a trans man (i.e. also assigned female at birth) who enjoys football would say 'I am a man and I enjoy football.'

For the majority of people (cis-gendered) assignment and

gender identity coincide. Cis-gendered people are comfortable with the sex characteristics of their bodies and, whilst they might not conform to socially constructed gender stereotypes, they do not feel they are the opposite gender, neither gender, or both genders.

Being gender variant means that someone does not identify with or relate to the sex characteristics they were born with and the societal expectations that are placed upon them due to their sex characteristics. The gender variant person might also feel averse to one or more of their sexual characteristics such as their penis or their breasts. This is known as gender dysphoria. Not everyone who expresses gender variance has gender dysphoria.

Developing non-binary approaches to gender and sexuality

People who identify with neither gender or both are starting to use the term non-binary gender. This term is being recognised to varying extents throughout the world. Currently Australia, New Zealand, India, Nepal, Pakistan, Argentina, Denmark and Malta all allow gender-neutral birth certificates, passports, or other official documentation.

However, even within the trans community some find this move towards non-binary gender by people who identify other than as the gender they were born with troubling. Such opponents feel that after a struggle it is a huge achievement to be female or male and they do not want that compromised in any way.

The experiences of those who are born with female sex

characteristics and those born with male are also different in the process of transition. Nathan talks of their trans men friends feeling guilty because of the way they are treated by society once they 'pass' as male. Nathan describes how they now feel safer walking alone at night, that as an apparent man they are now given more space, listened to much more and asked their opinions. They are aware that no matter how different they look, with their androgynous clothes, eye make-up and nail varnish, men still think they have something in common with them. Nathan thinks it wrong that they are now treated better than women.

When I was interviewing Colin about his relationship with his brother since the transition, he said that Nathan is 'just Nathan, without a gender'. When I asked him if he thought Nathan would be treated the same by society as before their transition, he at first said he thought yes until I reminded him all he had learned on his Politics and Social Policy course about female oppression and the need for feminism. He was surprised that he had not considered this nor reflected that in meetings with predominantly female colleagues it is often the men who talk more.

If anything, I feel Nathan has become *more* feminist and supportive of women since their transition. They have witnessed at first hand male privilege. This is now something they can 'enjoy' presenting as a white, middle-class profess-ional man, albeit one who is disabled.

Male to female trans adults have a harder job 'passing' due to height and the impact of testosterone. A small man does not attract the same attention as an unusually tall woman. If they do manage to pass as female they then have the added ignominy of being treated like cis-women (women who identify with their biological sex), and are thus subject to sexual harassment, oppression and lower social status. The idea that any man would choose to go down this route, with the sole intention of accessing women's safe spaces, as some feminists including a friend of mine argue, seems bizarre. One trans man I have spoken to believes that the patriarchal social construct we live in values maleness above all else, so that becoming a woman is seen as 'sick' in a way that a woman becoming male is not. Thus a man becoming a woman is seen as demotion. There has to be much more education from an early age so that this type of prejudice and discrimination against cis and trans women becomes socially unacceptable.

Other adults I have had the privilege of interviewing for this book have identified variously on the transgender spectrum: some don't want to be a man but don't identify as a woman either. Some want to be seen as a trans man or a trans woman, while others don't.

I discussed my feelings of distress about Nathan becoming a man with Oliver who then reflected on his own estrangement from his mother. She was a carer, looking after his dad who suffered from a variety of chronic impairments and like me had depended on her oldest daughter to meet her own emotional needs. Suffering from depression, she was distraught when Oliver came out as lesbian aged 15. With hindsight and as a result of our conversation, he reflected that his mum felt she had lost him then and that the gender variance had been an adjustment too far for her. She died before they had been able to regain their previous closeness.

Theories and models to help families stay well

My colleague Claire and I developed a model during our time at SNIP when we were working with the parents of disabled children. It is called the 3 As – acknowledge, adjust and adapt. We felt that too many professionals overemphasised the importance of parental 'acceptance' of their child's impairment. We felt this word implied a degree of approval of the situation, which many parents did not feel. We also felt that it implied that coming to terms with the realities of our child's condition was a one-off event. In contrast we knew that parents went through an ongoing process as their children grew up. We sought to redress this by presenting an alternative narrative around this process, thus coming up with the 3As as a way for parents to make sense of their thoughts and feelings. I think that this same model can be used by parents of transgender children and young people to navigate their emotions.

Parents first need to *acknowledge* what is happening. This means being able to state that their child is transgender, believe that it is in fact the case and understand the implications.

They then start to *adjust* to the reality of their child's life and let go of expectations that they consciously and sub-consciously had, based on what they thought their child's gender was.

Next they *adapt* their behaviour to the reality of their child's gender identity. For example, they can use the child's new name and adopt the appropriate pronouns. This process will possibly be repeated throughout the child's life as the impact of their transgenderism on the parents is evoked at particular stages, such as when cis-gendered friends of the child get married and start families.

When working with parents of disabled children we found that parents could better identify what was going on for them emotionally when they were encouraged to consider if their feelings were caused by an issue with acknowledging, adjusting or adapting.

For parents of transgender children this could mean for example: problems with acknowledging – grief for the loss of the alternative gendered child; problems with adjusting – perhaps distress at realising there would be no father and son bonding over pints at the pub; or problems with adapting – possible anger at having to constantly remember to use a name that they had not chosen. This separating out of the various stages can be useful for parents as it helps them to avoid becoming overwhelmed by their feelings.

In 1987 the journalist Jo Brans and sociologist Margaret Taylor Smith published a book based on the latter's sociological research. It is called *Mother, I have something to tell you* and in it they examine the response of traditional (American) mothers to their adult children's 'unexpected', 'untraditional' and often 'unacceptable' behaviour. Although this book is not specifically about gender identity issues, I found the six stage model they devised to explain the coping process mothers go through useful in making sense of what I was experiencing:

Stage 1 is *shock,* where the mother 'feels an
overwhelming sense of responsibility and guilt'.

Stage 2 is *attention*, where the mother learns to see 'the real child who exists under the ideal child she had created in her mind'.

Stage 3 is *action*, where the mother 'looks for help for herself, for her child and for the other members of the family' in order to understand and to cope.

Stage 4 is *detachment*, where the mother 'recognises the limits of her responsibility. . . and frees her child from her expectations of him or her'.

Stage 5 is *autonomy*, where the mother 'turns back to the only life for which she is completely responsible – her own'.

Stage 6 is *connection*, where the mother forges a new bond with the child and (or) with the world.

The authors write that the achievement of detachment – emotional, physical and financial – begins when a mother can recognise 'that her child is not herself' and that 'she can neither control nor make sense' of all that happens to him or her. This makes complete sense to me and helped me let go of the unrealistic expectations I had of myself as having to be the perfect mother.

The impact of grief and loss

Another model we used at SNIP was one we adapted from Jenni Thomas's work with parents of dying babies and children. From my experience I know that this applies equally well for what family members of transgender people are going through.

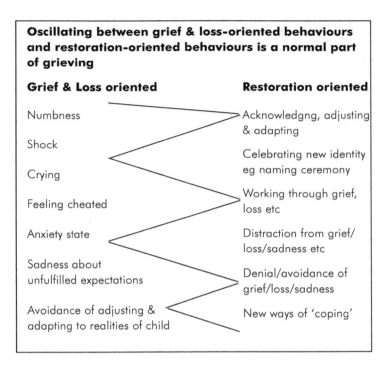

Oscillating between grief & loss-oriented behaviours and restoration-oriented behaviours is a normal part of grieving

Grief & Loss oriented   **Restoration oriented**

Numbness   Acknowledgng, adjusting
                                             & adapting

Shock   Celebrating new identity
                                             eg naming ceremony
Crying
                                             Working through grief,
Feeling cheated   loss etc

Anxiety state   Distraction from grief/
                                             loss/sadness etc
Sadness about
unfulfilled expectations   Denial/avoidance of
                                             grief/loss/sadness

Avoidance of adjusting &   New ways of 'coping'
adapting to realities of child

It can help people enormously if they understand that each parent (and indeed the trans child, siblings, extended family and friends) is going through this process of oscillation which is normal but extremely challenging. Recognising that on any one day some of the family might be adopting grief- and loss-oriented behaviour whilst another wakes up feeling restorative can explain why people who have previously been able to support each other are unable to do so at this time. When one person is feeling overwhelmed by grief, they cannot bear to be around their partner or child who is breezing about the house apparently 'over' the loss. Likewise, to wake up feeling positive about the future and be faced by someone who cannot stop crying is hugely challenging. This means that grief, rather than bringing people together, can push them away from each other, further adding to their distress.

Parents of trans sons and daughters often feel they are in some way betraying them if they talk about their own grief and loss. This means parents can become trapped in their grief state and leads them into depression. It is very important, therefore, that a safe place is available for them to express their true feelings away from their offspring. The same is also true for siblings.

CHAPTER 7
Language

I use a number of terms throughout this book which I now explain more fully in this chapter. I use the terms that children, young people and adults whose stories are included in the book employ to describe themselves. I respect their wishes regarding the use of pronouns.

Sex – This refers to the labels given to babies at birth based on a brief assessment of their physical characteristics, such as external genitalia. Sex is traditionally divided into the categories of male and female, but physical sex characteristics are much more diverse (see intersex definition).

Gender identity – According to the Yogyakarta Principles (outlined by a team of international lawyers in 2006 in Indonesia), gender identity refers to each person's deeply felt internal and individual experience of gender, which may or may not correspond with the sex assigned at birth.

Transgender – This is an umbrella term for those whose gender identity or expression differs in some way from the sex assigned to them at birth and also conflicts with the norms society expects of people of that sex. Included in the overall transgender umbrella are male to female people, female to male people, non-binary people and people who cross-dress.

Non-binary gender – Gender identities that are not exclusively male or female are identities which are outside of the gender binary. People can be both male and female, neither female nor male, their gender may be more fluid (i.e. unfixed and changeable over the course of time), or they feel genderless.

Cross-dressing – This refers to wearing clothing typical of the opposite sex. People who cross dress generally identify with their sex assigned at birth.

Intersex – This applies to a person whose chromosomes, reproductive organs or genitalia vary in some way from what is traditionally considered clearly male or female. This may be apparent at birth or become apparent later in life, often at puberty, or when they try to conceive.

Cis – A cis person is someone who identifies as the same gender they were designated at birth. So if someone is born female and identifies as a woman, they are cis. Using this term is an attempt to avoid positioning cis people as 'the norm'.

Sexual orientation – People sometimes confuse gender identity with sexual orientation and, as a result, think that trans is another category of sexual orientation or sexuality. Trans, however, describes how you feel about your gender identity only. Trans people can be straight, gay, bisexual, or something else entirely, just like everyone else.

Straight – This term refers to people who are attracted to people who identify as the opposite gender to themselves.

Gay/lesbian – Gay men and lesbian women are attracted to people who identify as the same gender as them.

Bisexual – Bisexual people are attracted to people who identify as the same gender as them and to people who identify as a different gender to them.

Queer – This is an umbrella term used by people who identify their sexuality as something other than straight.

Transitioning – Transitioning describes the journey from female to male or male to female (or to something else entirely!). This may or may not be through taking hormones or having surgical intervention.

Coming out – This refers to the act of disclosing your sexuality, trans status or gender identity to another person.

Gender binary – The idea/social construct in some cultures (including Scotland and the rest of the Western world) is that there are only two genders – male and female. People who see themselves as non-binary feel they are outside of these categories.

Transphobia – Transphobia is the fear or dislike of someone who identifies as trans.

Homophobia – The irrational hatred, intolerance, and fear of lesbian, gay and bisexual people.

Biphobia – The irrational hatred, intolerance, and fear of people particularly because of their bisexuality – often perpetuated by negative stereotypes such as that bi people are 'greedy' or 'should make up their minds'.

CHAPTER 8
Is Scotland leading the way for trans and non-binary gender people?

The Scottish Transgender Alliance and the Equality Network, various other LGBT organisations and trans people themselves have worked tirelessly over the past few years with the Scottish Government and the Scottish Parliament to develop legislative and policy changes. According to the Trans Rights Europe Index 2016 this ostensibly makes Scotland one of the best places in Europe to be trans or non-binary.

In this chapter I look at these various developments and share the stories of other trans and non-binary adults, children/young people and their families to see if the lived reality of people matches that positive narrative.

In Scotland, as in the rest of the UK and the US, there are increasing numbers of people identifying as gender variant as children, in teenage years and at various stages in adulthood. Any support must therefore be provided across the age range and also be available for their parents, who might be in their 20s or 80s. Equally their siblings could be toddlers or pensioners.

In the current social climate, one in three marriages end in divorce and there are high rates of remarriage or people having 'second families'. So there is the added complexity of parents of younger children who may have differing views on the right way to handle their child's gender variance.

Some parents of trans people themselves identify in a variety of ways around gender and this can be extremely positive. For instance, one of my interviewees, Adam describes his mum's trans man partner as having been 'a great role model and support'.

Faith

As gender is context specific, religious beliefs held by families have a huge impact on the way in which they respond to their son or daughter coming out as trans. Although church attendance continues to fall in Scotland, the 2011 Census showed that 63 per cent of respondents described themselves as having faith, so religion must still affect a significant proportion of families. With an increasingly diverse population, those providing services in Scotland need to understand the needs of people from all faiths (or none) and cultures.

Rebecca, a trainee psychotherapist and care worker, of mixed cultural heritage was brought up in Ireland within the Greek and Russian Orthodox Church. Rebecca told me: 'I don't want to be a man and I don't identify as a woman, specifically I have a dysphoria around my breasts. I draw on psychotherapy to make sense of myself.'

They go on to say: 'There are expectations to be very feminine in the Russian Orthodox Church. I had to wear a dress and remember feeling "this isn't right, this is an assault". I now identify as aethist, feeling that I was not accepted within the church community and relating that to being female. I feel my queer identity is more related to being atheist.'

Rebecca describes a background of living in a home where they were the black sheep of the family and seeking out other families to replace their own. Their mother is hyper-critical, having her own issues of repulsion, confusion and envy resulting from her relationship with her own mother.

They and their partner Tara discuss that it would be hard for Tara's parents to get their heads around the fact that their daughter is in a lesbian relationship with a woman who wants to look like a man. Tara's family speak Russian – a language which is totally gendered and has no such word as 'partner' so Tara must introduce Rebecca as her girlfriend.

Coming out as a mature adult with a partner

Mia was born apparently male and talks about hiding in a cupboard from about age 5, knowing she was female and putting on tights and skirts taken from her sister's drawers. She would also take Barbie dolls into the cupboard to play with. She says that she hated her body because it did not fit with her gender. She was very involved with the arts and just told people she was 'in touch with her feminine side' and trawled the charity shops for bright, highly patterned 1960s flared trousers and shirts. In her early twenties she persuaded herself that she was only going through a phase and got married and became a father. Sadly after a few year's Mia's wife died and she regrets bitterly that she did not tell her wife that she was transgender before her death. Mia told her current partner Sarah not long after they moved in together. Initially Mia said that she wanted to share clothes and makeup with Sarah and then within a couple of days she told her that she is a woman. Mia has always loved brightly patterned clothes but because of her job she has to wear male clothes at work, which is making life difficult for her.

Sarah wasn't against Mia's identifying as a woman, but wasn't sure they'd survive as a couple. She has found it stressful but they are negotiating their relationship and Sarah's parents have been totally supportive. Recognising the courage it takes for Mia to be who she needs to be, Sarah's father told Mia, 'I loved you before and I love you even more now'.

Now in her late thirties, Mia has only just felt able to 'come out' as a woman. She is clear she is a woman and rejects the term trans. She describes the hassle she gets when out, with men shouting at her but on principle is not comfortable with the development of a trans community as she feels this perpetuates stigma. She is currently on the year long waiting list for her first assessment at the Gender Identity Clinic. She is taking hormones privately and looking forward to getting her surgery.

Mia did not discuss any of this with her family until she started her transition process. She is now struggling with her sister's response as she didn't speak to Mia for six months. Her sister assumed that she liked men thus confusing gender and sexuality. This added to Mia's stress and anxiety about being accepted within the family. She wonders if her sister feels resentment at being ousted from her position as the only daughter and envious of the attention Mia is now getting.

Coming from a liberal, alternative family, Mia is really struggling with her mother's response. Like me, her mum had always expressed support for transgender people, but when she learned about Mia she said, 'it's all rubbish, you will look ridiculous'. Like other parents I have interviewed, Mia's parents feel that they 'would have known' and so dismiss what she is telling them. This is very hard for Mia. Her mum and dad are upset about losing their son and say they are fearful for her.

Understandably, Sarah finds it hard to hear these comments which are hurtful for her partner but can empathise with Mia's sister feeling usurped from her position within the family and her parents' shock and distress. She can see that they have not had the same length of time as Mia and Sarah have had to come to terms with what is happening.

On the bright side, all Mia's friends have been totally supportive and this has been wonderful for her.

Children and young people

This uniqueness of each trans adult and their family's experience that I have heard in my interviews epitomises the enormous challenge for parents with children identifying as gender variant. As I described in an earlier chapter, only a small number of children who appear to be gender variant in their early years go on to be trans. What young children need is the freedom to express themselves as they wish and not be bound by societal stereotypes that reinforce patriarchal norms of dominant, active masculinity and deferent, passive femininity.

I am therefore delighted to see that Scotland's Zero Tolerance organisation is developing an online gender equality training tool for those working in the early years, and to learn that at least one local authority is developing gender equal early years provision. This progress is alongside LGBT Youth Scotland's excellent collaboration with local authority equality officers and educational psychologists in developing guidance 'To offer supportive and practical information to all staff who work with children and young people in order to support young people who are or may be gay, lesbian, bisexual or transgender'.

This guidance sets support for these vulnerable pupils under the umbrella of the anti-bullying and prejudice agenda. It is a clear and accessible document that, alongside training, should give the answers to many of the questions those working with children and young people might have. It should also help them develop the confidence to challenge bullying and prejudice in various aspects of their lives.

Some local authorities are also providing training on unconscious bias which will help staff to understand their own deeply held prejudices and discriminatory beliefs so that they can address them. Whether or not we like to acknowledge it, all of us internalise societal influences. To be effective allies of our trans children all of us – young people, friends, family members, students, and work colleagues – need to work through and abandon those stereotypical views that are no longer helpful for our relationships and society.

Local authorities have an obligation to meet the needs of trans children and young people under the Scottish Government's policy framework 'Getting it Right for Every Child'

(GIRFEC). Where there are concerns for the child this requires professionals to assess whether the child's needs are being met under the headings of safe, healthy, included, nurtured, active, respected, and responsible. I sincerely hope that getting it right in schools will make a big difference to children experiencing gender variance/gender dysphoria and that working with children from a young age will ensure that future generations do not have to suffer the stigma that previous ones had to bear.

Children and young people are also included in the Additional Support for Learning legislation which means that if their learning is being affected by issues arising from their gender variance, then they should be assessed to ascertain what extra support would help them meet their potential.

As we know, children are not one dimensional and often don't simply have gender identity issues. Like Nathan they may also be disabled and/or have diagnosed or undiagnosed impairments which affect the ways they experience life. They may have differently wired brains, which mean that professionals have to work with them in different ways.

Implications for those also on the autistic spectrum

A consultant paediatrician who specialises in working with children and young people on the autistic spectrum talks about the added complication of what he calls 'intersectionality'. He uses this to describe the 'intersection' between someone's impairment, gender identity, race, culture and/or sexuality when they also identify as trans. Concrete and black and white thinking can be traits of those with autistic spectrum disorder and anyone parenting or anyone working with a child or young person with this combination needs to be aware that their condition might have an impact on the way they experience the transition process. These young people may find it intolerable to live with the uncertainty of the outcome of surgery or what impact hormone treatment could have on their bodies. One mum describes her trans son's huge distress when she repeatedly told him 'you are the same person to me'. This mum did feel that her trans son was the same person, regardless of his gender identity, but the child needed her to go with him to his 'real' self, which was male and, in his mind, this was not the same at all. This led to the poor mum unwittingly adding to her son's distress. She had the best of intentions and this highlights once again that one parental approach will not work for all trans people.

Marilyn Misandry is a 22 year old who identifies as a drag queen, transgender, femme, queer and autistic. In an article in *Diva* magazine Marilyn says:

> I . . . found that the dysphoria that often comes with living as a trans person was increasingly difficult with autism and still do. When autistics are taught coping skills, we are rarely thought of as existing as more than autistics. And often my autistic identity is used to undermine my queer and trans identity. But for me they are inseparable parts of myself, they make me Marilyn Misandry.

As I write, the Scottish Intercollegiate Guidelines Network (SIGN) is rewriting its guidelines on autistic spectrum disorder and gender dysphoria is covered within them for the first time. There is currently speculation, not sufficiently evidenced in research yet, that those on the autistic spectrum, many of whom do not feel the need to conform to social stereotypes, may be proportionally more likely to identify as trans or non-binary gender, androgynous or gender fluid. As the diagnosis of autistic spectrum disorder is also increasing every year, links between both spectrums need to be examined so that if someone presents on both they can access the right support.

Health services

In April 2014 the National Gender Identity Clinical Network for Scotland (NGICNS) was established to support Scotland's adoption of the Gender Reassignment Protocol (GRP). This is another very welcome development. GRP incorporates the recommendations from the 7th edition of The World Profess-ional Association for Transgender Health (WPATH) Standards of Care (September 2011). The key aim of this new network, one of a number of National Managed Clinical Networks (NMCNs) in Scotland, is to ensure there is equitable access to planned gender identity services, providing national person-centred support through stressful, life changing events for gender variant patients in Scotland.

Notwithstanding these excellent developments it still appears that in the eleven years since we as a family started on this journey parents across Scotland continue to describe their experience as full of stress, anxiety and isolation.

There is only one Gender Identity Clinic (GIC) in Scotland for children and young people which offers the full multi-disciplinary service required by the WPATH standards. This is at the Sandyford Clinic in Glasgow. This GIC is currently staffed by one psychiatrist working only half a week. This is for 700 patients. The number of patients being referred is doubling each year so, even with an extra half time psychiatric post, it is unlikely that Sandyford will be able to offer the quality service that the patients and their families need and deserve. As I write, there is the prospect of new staff starting at the clinic, but the rising demand – increasing 100 per cent year on year – means that waiting lists will still remain much higher than is desirable for children and young people in such distress.

What's more, GPs are often unaware of the Gender Reassignment Protocol and in some cases have sent families to the wrong place prior to them being referred onto a lengthy waiting list. This currently stands at a full year for a first assessment appointment. Although there is some cover in other NHS Board areas such as Highland and Lothian, these clinics do not offer the same experience for families. So travelling to Glasgow, which is both time-consuming and expensive, is often the only way for families to access the full range of services. Families faced with children and young people who are suffering mental distress, depression or anxiety due to their gender dysphoria are feeling compelled to go privately for treatment as we did ourselves. This does not fit with the stated aim of GINMCN to provide equitable acess for treatment.

Dangers facing trans people – the dilemma of being out

Dealing with the difficulties of accessing medical care is bad enough but when we add the knowledge parents have of the terrible realities faced by trans people throughout the world, such as suicide and murder victim rates, it is little wonder that that they struggle to cope. Trying to defeat stigma, yet being fearful of the dangers that exist for your child if they are 'out' is another form of cognitive dissonance faced by parents and indeed trans people themselves.

Minority groups hope that by personalising stigmatising issues, we will appeal to people's humanity and sense that this could be happening to my family or me. This is what lesbian, gay and bisexual people have done with great effect in Scotland over the past three decades. For trans people, this is still in its infancy, for very understandable reasons. Copious media coverage of the issues leads us to believe that attitudes towards trans people have greatly improved but they haven't. In fact in some parts of the world, most notably in the USA, hard won rights for transgender people are being overthrown. This means that being the parent of a trans child, young person or adult is fraught with the dilemma of whether to be open about what's happening in your family. For example, if as a parent you talk on social media about your child being transgender you may be unwittingly 'outing' your child against their best interests, now and for years to come. This is also true for other family members.

It is telling that apart from our family, no-one whose story appears in this book has felt willing to reveal their real name or initials. On paper Scotland may look like a great place for trans people and relative to other countries this may be so, but the lived reality of trans people compared to cis-gendered people shows there is still much to be done.

Family stories

Toni

Toni is the mum of a 12 year old child, Nick, who is currently socially transitioning into being a boy. Toni describes feeling so isolated that she sometimes fantasises about running away. She has been receiving some support from a parent support group and a worker at LGBT Youth Scotland but she is having a difficult time. Her former husband and Nick's father is opposed to Toni supporting Nick to make this transition both socially and through the use of hormone blockers. Nick is on a lengthy waiting list at the Sandyford Gender Identity Clinic for these drugs. Toni's ex-husband is verbally abusive to her and she feels she needs to avoid school meetings about Nick when she thinks he will be there. This is greatly adding to Toni's stress at the long wait for Nick's hormone treatment. She has been offered counselling through the Sandyford clinic and although she feels this would be useful, the long journey to Glasgow, if she isn't combining it with other appointments, makes it an unattractive option.

Toni says she really values participating in the parent group, especially as it is not only her former husband who is opposing what she is doing: she feels some of her good friends are judging her and getting her to question whether she is doing the right thing.

Yet research shows that 86 per cent of trans adolescents report they have improved mental health when they are prescribed hormone blockers. These blockers reduce the impact of puberty on secondary sex characteristics. This reduces the distress for the pubescent young person who doesn't want to suffer the trauma of their body changing even more into what they feel is the wrong sex. However, these drugs are not without potential side effects and this has to be weighed against the benefits when a young person or their carer is deciding whether or not to have them prescribed.

Toni describes feeling rejected and hurt in the same way as I was, when her daughter, prior to talking about the need to transition, was not enthusiastic to talk about getting her first bra or starting periods. However, Toni is now embracing Nick's transition and is preparing for his coming out at school. The school staff have had training and he is starting to tell friends, as is his sister. They are planning a naming ceremony complete with banners declaring 'It's a boy!' and gifts displaying his new name. On his recent birthday relatives sent him cards reflecting his new gender identity. Both Nick and Toni really appreciated this gesture. Nick has also written a rap to perform at the party in which talks about being trans.

Diane

Diane is also estranged from her trans son's father. She describes her distress and feelings of despair when her son Sam was sectioned under the Mental Health Act due to his emotional meltdowns and suicide attempts. When I heard Diane describing her son I wondered if he might have Asperger's Syndrome as well as gender dysphoria. Sam's psychiatrist has now raised the question of Asperger's with Diane and she says it makes sense of her son's behaviour when he was growing up.

David and Susan

When I visited David and Susan they told me that their trans daughter, Mhairi, had broken the news to them just as they arrived home from New Zealand following their holiday of a lifetime. Another of their three children had persuaded Mhairi to wait until their return to make this disclosure. They recall the shock and numbness on hearing this news – shock heightened by jet lag and the usual feelings of disorientation after a long flight and time away from home. David talks about 'a lot of shouting and tears' that night as they heard that their son had been hiding female clothes in his room since he was about 12. They recount that Mhairi wanted to rip up all the pictures of her as a child and their relief that she resisted this. Susan describes feelings very similar to mine. She also had a difficult experience when accessing support. David commented that he felt 'it is the mums who feel it more, dads are just the support. . .' He says he can only think of Mhairi as female and looks at her 'as a person'.

Susan describes a difficult time between her and Mhairi in the year or so following her disclosure, when it became necessary for both of them that Mhairi left the family home and moved into her own flat.

Support

Thankfully, alongside the growing population of children, young people and adults identifying as trans, parent support groups are starting to be established in Scotland. Private Facebook groups can provide a way for parents and trans people themselves to keep in touch between meetings. They also provide a way of being involved for those who, by virtue of geographical distance, disability or other barriers cannot access face-to-face meetings. TransParentsees runs two such groups, one in Glasgow and one in Edinburgh. These recently established, and highly regarded, parent led groups offer parents the safe space they need to share, not only their thoughts and feelings about parenting their trans children or young people, but also hints and tips about treatment options and so forth.

Furthermore, LGBT Health has just held a very successful family day, when the trans children, together with their parents and siblings, were able to meet together, relaxed in the knowledge that everyone understood what they were going through.

Not all parents will find groups useful, however. So it is also important that one-to-one support is available for those who may find themselves unable to speak up for fear that their concerns are somehow less valid than others. Sometimes people over-empathise with other parents who are going through a bad time and therefore come out feeling worse than when they went in!

CHAPTER 9
Conclusions and recommendations

As can be seen from the life stories presented in this book, the lives of trans and gender variant people and their families in Scotland are complex and complicated.

Nevertheless, there are common feelings of loss, grief, shock, disbelief, fear, embarrassment, guilt and shame. But there is also joy, relief, contentment, success, achievement and hope. Most of all, threaded throughout all these stories is love. Love by trans people for their families, even when they are struggling with the length of time it takes for their parents and siblings to come to terms with who they really are. Love from parents, siblings, extended family and friends for trans people. Love expressed in a myriad of practical and emotional ways.

But the stories also highlight the stresses and pressures families are under. Parents simultaneously need to be there for their children as well as provide for them. Everyday life has to go on, regardless of a child being sick, disabled or gender non-conforming. If the parents themselves are sick or disabled, caring for their elderly parents or whatever, this can also put parents' relationships with each other, their children, their extended family and friends under incredible strain. It can also compromise their ability to be good employees.

Ian and I are aware that we are privileged as we could continue to earn income when other parents cannot. Nonetheless we still struggled emotionally and psychologically. So for those with multiple problems it is vitally important that more support is provided. I would like to see an allowance for families of trans children, young people and adults to meet the increased costs that are not met by Health Boards. This would help with travel to appointments, restocking wardrobes, childcare for younger siblings and so forth, thus alleviating some of this added financial pressure.

Making Scotland the best place to be transgender

In addition there are a number of other ways to improve the lived experience of trans people and their families. All the recommendations I list below have been supported wholeheartedly by all those I spoke to for this book. In most cases these recommendations would need to be taken forward by the Scottish Government, however academic institutions, funding bodies such as the Big Lottery Fund, voluntary sector organisations and philanthropists could all make a valuable contribution.

■ Build on current good practice to extend family-focussed approaches to support (including when the trans person is an adult, if that is what they want) via the provision of facilitative, therapeutic processes for family members, individually and collectively according to each family's needs, to help each member make sense of what they are thinking and feeling.

■   Commission an urgent review of the resourcing of Gender Identity Clinics to reduce waiting lists and provide a quality service to patients and their families.

■   Establish a centre, or centres, which family members, collectively and individually can use as a retreat to grieve and regroup. Such centres could be modelled on children's hospices, which provide a variety of therapeutic inputs under one roof for all family members. The value of families meeting others, together with professional support is well evidenced.

Professional development

■   Provide a strategic level training programme across all health boards and local authorities, which is properly resourced and embedded in college level, undergraduate and postgraduate study for anyone working with people, together with appropriate continuous professional development.

■   Provide the type of training outlined above particularly for general practitioners and others in primary care so that they can become more aware of the issues facing trans people and their families. This would reduce the distress they go through prior to arriving at the Gender Identity Clinic.

Research

■ Commission a longitudinal study of the cohort of children identifying with gender variance/trans/ gender dysphoria to track their outcomes including whether or not it is best to give hormone suppressing treatment.

■ Commission research into the true cost of parenting a transgender child as well as the economic costs facing those who are transgender adults.

■ Commission a sociological study on how the 'pinkification' and genderising of clothes, toys and accessories, the hypersexualisation of girls, and the exponential growth of pornography are affecting the gender identity development of children and young people.

Public awareness

■ Reduce the impact of being trans or gender variant by gender neutralising public spaces. Persuade the media to refrain from using language that perpetuates gender stereotyping and reinforces prejudice and discrimination.

■ Extend gender neutral early years provision so that it is available across the public, voluntary and private sectors.

■ Increase the representation of trans people in public life so that trans children and young people have positive role models.

He, She, They

REFERENCES AND HELPFUL INFORMATION

References in the text

Carrie Lyell, *Diva*, March 2016.

Judy Voirst, *Imperfect Control*, Fireside, New York, 1999.

Christina Wieland, *The Undead Mother: Psychoanalytic explorations of masculinity, femininity and matricide*, Rebus Press, London, 2002.

The City of Edinburgh Council & LGBT Youth Scotland, 'Supporting Transgender, Lesbian, Gay and Bisexual Young People in our Services', 2015.

Resources that helped me

Compassionate Mind Therapy – Paul Gilbert, *The Compassionate Mind*, Constable & Robinson, London, 2009.

Mindfulness – Eckhart Toll, *The Power of Now*, Hodder & Stoughton, London, 2001.

Cognitive Behavioural Therapy – Rob Willson & Rhena Branch, *Cognitive Behavioural Therapy for Dummies*, John Wiley & Sons, Chichester, 2010.

Useful contacts

Scottish Transgender Alliance
Working to improve gender identity and gender
reassignment equality, rights and inclusion in Scotland.

http://www.scottishtrans.org

Equality Network
Scotland's national lesbian, gay, bisexual, transgender and
intersex (LGBTI) equality and human rights charity.

http://equality-network.org

National Gender Identity Managed Clinical Network
(NGIMCN)
NGIMCN aims to work with gender identity clinics, gender
reassignment surgical providers, primary care, patient and
third sector representation to achieve timely, coordinated,
service provision and equitable access to planned gender
identity clinical services across Scotland.

To achieve these aims NGICNS will bring together service
users, health care professionals, gender identity service
providers, parents, carers, young people and voluntary
sector groups interested in providing gender services.

www.ngicns.scot.nhs.uk

Gender Identity Research and Education Society
Information for trans people, their families and the
professionals who care for them.

http://www.gires.org.uk

LGBT Youth Scotland
Youth and community-based organisation for lesbian, gay,
bisexual and transgender (LGBT) people in Scotland,
providing access to help or advice when young people
need it. At the time of writing, LGBT Youth Scotland are in
the process of developing specific and broader guidance
about supporting transgender young people in schools, in
partnership with Scottish Transgender Alliance and other
education sector organisations.

https://www.lgbtyouth.org.uk

LGBT Health & Wellbeing Scotland
Promoting the health, wellbeing and equality of lesbian,
gay, bisexual and transgender (LGBT) people in Scotland.

http://www.lgbthealth.org.uk

Mermaids

UK-wide organisation providing family and individual support for teenagers and children with gender identity issues.

http://www.mermaidsuk.org.uk

TransparenTsees

West of Scotland:
This parent support group runs on the first Thursday of the month from 6pm till 7.45pm. Venue is in the meeting room on the top floor at Sandyford Counselling and Support Service (SCASS) at Sauchiehall Street, 2-6 Sandyford Place, Glasgow G3 7NB. If you would like to find out more, please email transparentsees@gmail.com.

East of Scotland:
The first East of Scotland Group was held on 1st February 2016, 6pm until 8pm, in the LGBT Youth Scotland offices, Citadel House, 40 Commercial Street, Leith, EH6 6JD. Thereafter, the group will be held on the first Monday of every month. Please contact transparentsees@gmail.com for more details.

Kindred

Kindred provides advocacy and information on services available to children with additional support needs and their carers. You don't always have to have a specific question for the organisation as they also provide a 'listening ear'.

www.kindred-scotland.org

National Autistic Society Scotland

This is the leading UK charity for autistic people (including those with Asperger's syndrome) and their families.

They provide information, support and pioneering services, and campaign for a better world for autistic people.

www.autism.org.uk

Zero Tolerance

Zero Tolerance is a Scottish charity working to end men's violence against women by promoting gender equality and by challenging attitudes which normalise violence and abuse.

www.zerotolerance.org.uk

AFTERWORD

by Nathan Gale

When my mum first raised the idea of writing a book about the impact of my transition on our family I instinctively said yes. I don't feel I have ownership of our story. It's just as much mum's to tell as it is mine. The idea of our family's experience being out there for other people to read excited me for another reason: I think it's important for us all to hear various stories about trans people's lives. It was probably this enthusiasm that stopped me from thinking deeply about how mum writing the book, and then people reading it, would actually make me feel.

When I sat down to read the first draft, the biggest surprise was how little of the early part of my transition I could remember. I'm not sure whether this was because I'd suppressed what was a pretty terrible time or simply because it was over a decade ago and remembering last week can be a challenge. But either way, when mum and I started to talk about the early years after my coming out it almost felt as if we were talking about someone else's life.

These were challenging discussions but I'm glad we persevered and I was able to engage more with the journey we had been on as a family. For the first time since I transitioned I was able to look at photos from my childhood and not feel guilt or shame. Reading about how my family had experienced things finally enabled me to let go of the narrative I had about my transition and to replace it with one which was much more compassionate towards my younger self. Indeed this is just one of the reasons why I am so grateful to my mum for writing this book.

I never had any doubt that the book would be published. When my mum decides to do something she makes sure it gets done. I'm so incredibly proud of the work she has put in to telling our story and giving a voice to other families who have had experiences similar to ours. I couldn't possibly have imagined when I drunkenly came out to her on my 20th birthday that all these years later she would be proudly recounting how resilient, supportive and loving our family is.

Nor could mum and I have imagined when she first started writing the book how much higher up the Scottish government's agenda trans rights would be. At the end of the book my mum makes a number of recommendations to improve the lives of trans young people and their families and, given the prominence of these issues now, such advice is appropriate and timely.

I sincerely hope that the book can do two things. First, raise awareness of how much better outcomes could be if families are given the support they so desperately need. And second encourage families to love their transitioning child as I have been loved by my family. Loved, not in spite of the fact they are trans. Loved because being trans has made them who they are.

September 2016

ACKNOWLEDGEMENTS

First and foremost I am indebted to Ian, Nathan, Colin, Robert and Brittany for allowing me to write so honestly and openly about our family's experiences.

I would also like to thank all the other trans and non-binary gender people and their families for sharing their stories with me. They have been so generous, hoping as I do that the book will help others going through similar experiences and contribute to reducing the stigma around gender identity issues.

To all those who contributed to the book from the perspective of supporting trans people and their families, in voluntary and professional capacities I thank you. Not just for those contributions, but also for the work you do with people who are still some of the most stigmatised and vulnerable in Scotland.

When I read Carol Craig's call for women writers for the Postcards series it felt like a gift. I am immensely grateful to her for her enthusiasm for the subject, followed up with her skilful and supportive editing. I'm also grateful for her coming up with the title, which we struggled with. I also want to thank everyone involved in the Centre for Confidence and Well-being for publishing the book. Thank you to Pete Fletcher for producing a great cover in (co-incidentally) Nathan's favourite colour.

I am delighted that writing the book has also brought me into contact with Elaine Henry at Word Power books. I am grateful to her for our lively discussions about the title and for featuring the book at the Edinburgh Independent Radical Book Fair.

I couldn't have written the book without the ongoing support of Rachel Henry, my brilliant practice supervisor in the day job, who helped me to see I could incorporate other families' stories to make a book with broader relevance, nor Diane McKay who has helped me live better with my Post Traumatic Stress Disorder.

I would like to thank everyone who was alongside Nathan, Colin, Ian and myself during what were some of our darkest moments: our extended families, especially Raymond, Pat, the late Bill and Caz; our many friends, for support that continues, in particular Carol and Errol, Paula and Walter, Skeatsey, Kim, Lindy Lou, Cath, Leigh, Morag, Janet and Fi. I would like to extend huge thanks to Lesley and Diana for lending me places to weep. To Carol in Buffalo, USA, thanks for providing me with a refuge when the grief was over-whelming

To my incomparable staff team at SNIP – Claire, Sharon, Veronica, Helen and Margaret – I can never thank you enough for keeping the amazing service to families going in my absence. To the wonderful SNIP Board, especially Carrie Upton, thank you for your compassion and support that enabled me to keep my job.

To all my colleagues at the Family Fund, Education Scotland and the Big Lottery Fund, thank you for your support when things felt grim and for encouraging me to draw on my parenting experiences appropriately and effectively in my public appointments.

Lastly, thanks to my newer friends who have only known me since Nathan's transition and who have been a big part of my recovery – Karen and family, Gerry and everyone at No Strings Attached Wind Band.

1. AfterNow – What next for a healthy Scotland?
| *Phil Hanlon/Sandra Carlisle*
The authors of this visionary book look at health in Scotland and
beyond health to the main social, economic, environmental and
cultural challenges of our times. They examine the type of
transformational change required to create a more resilient and
healthy Scotland.

2. The Great Takeover – How materialism, the media and
markets now dominate our lives | *Carol Craig*
Describes the dominance of materalist values, the media and
business in all our lives and how this is leading to a loss of
individual and collective well-being. It looks at many of the big
issues of our times – debt, inequality, political apathy, loss of self-
esteem, pornography and the rise of celebrity culture. The
conclusion is simple and ultimately hopeful – we can change our
values and our lives.

3. The New Road – Charting Scotland's inspirational
communities | *Alf Young/Ewan Young*
A father and son go on a week long journey round Scotland to
see at first hand some of the great environmental, social,
employment and regeneration projects which are happening.
From Dunbar in the south east of Scotland to Knoydart in the
north west they meet people involved in projects which
demonstrate new ways of living.

4. Scotland's Local Food Revolution | *Mike Small*
Lifts the lid on the unsavoury reality of our current food system
including horsemeat in processed beef products, the
unsustainable movement of food round the globe, and how
supermarket shopping generates massive waste. It's an
indictment of a food syste that is out of control. But there is hope
– the growth and strength of Scotland's local food movement.

5. Letting Go – Breathing new life into organisations
| *Tony Miller/Gordon Hall*
It is now commonplace for employees to feel frustrated at work –
ground down by systems that are dominated by rules, protocols,
guidelines, targets and inspections. Tony Miller and Gordon Hall
explore the origins of 'command and control' management as
well as the tyranny of modern day 'performance management'.
Effective leaders, they argue, should 'let go' of their ideas on
controlling staff and nurture intrinsic motivation instead.

6. Raising Spirits – Allotments, well-being and community |
Jenny Mollison/Judy Wilkinson/Rona Wilkinson
Allotments are the unsung story of our times; hidden places for
food, friendship and freedom from the conformity of everyday
life. A fascinating look at how allotments came about; why they
can make such a substantial contribution to health, well-being,
community, food production, and the environment; and what's
happening in other countries.

7. Schooling Scotland – Education, equity and community |
Daniel Murphy
The Scottish schooling system does well for many children
growing up in Scotland, but to ensure that all children get the
education they deserve, a better partnership of parent, child,
school, government and society is needed – one to which all
Scotland can contribute and from which all children can benefit.
Daniel Murphy suggests eight ways to ensure that Scottish
education could be stronger and fairer.

8. Shaping our Global Future – A guide for young people | *Derek Brown*
Young people worry about the future world they will live in: personal futures, families and jobs. But they also worry about their global futures. The possibilities and challenges ahead appear overwhelming. This guide to human achievements and future challenges is designed to help young people consider the future their children and grandchildren will inhabit.

9. Conviction – Violence, culture and a shared public service agenda | *John Carnochan*
Policeman John Carnochan takes us on a memorable journey of discovery as he comes to grips with violence and Scotland's traditionally high murder rate. He also gives a fascinating insight into the work of Scotland's Violence Reduction Unit and why it has been so spectacularly successful. This compelling book is not about high visibility policing or more officers but the importance of empathy and children's early years.

10. She, He, They – Families, gender and coping with transition | *Shirley Young*
How challenging can gender transition be for both parents and siblings? A story of hope and resilience, it shows that if parents can move beyond the shock and pain of their offspring's transition, all family members can come closer together and experience life-enhancing change.

11. Knowing and Growing – Insights for developing ourselves and others | *Alan McLean*
This extraordinary book provides insights and practical tools to help you navigate everyday human interactions, balance your own and others' needs and utilise your emotions to create a more fulfilling life. The powerful insights readers glean from 'McLean's Ring' are not only helpful for parents, teachers and leaders they are also essential for anyone aiming to encourage others to grow and develop as individuals.

12. Working for Equality – Policy, politics people |
Richard Freeman, Fiona McHardy, Danny Murphy (Editors)
Brings together 22 experienced practitioners from across the country to reflect on equality/inequality – in class, race, gender, poverty, disability and homelessness as well as health and education. They are concerned about individuals as well as ideas and policy instruments. Short and accessible, a pause for thought and inspiration for those concerned with action.

13. Hiding in Plain Sight – Exploring Scotland's ill health
| *Carol Craig*
Scotland. A country that prides itself on its modernity and progressive instincts. Yet this is a nation whose mental and physical health outcomes are poor by European standards. This book asks why? Grippingly readable yet challenging, Carol Craig offers an answer which is glaringly obvious. Generations of Scottish children have suffered in ways that undermine the nation's health. Starting from her own and her neighbours' lives, she explores the growing awareness internationally of the impact of Adverse Childhood Experiences.

14. Right from the Start – Investing in parents and babies
| *Alan Sinclair*
Scotland languishes in the second division of global child well-being. One child in every four is judged to be 'vulnerable' when they enter primary school. Alan Sinclair reveals the harm inflicted on so many of our youngest, most defenceless citizens through a toxic mix of poor parenting, bad health and a society focussed on dealing with consequences rather than causes. He also sets out a routemap for us to start putting children first by helping us all to become better parents.

15. The Golden Mean – fostering young people's resilience, confidence and well-being | *Morag Kerr (Editor)*
How do we encourage children and young people and help foster the skills they need to thrive in our increasingly complex world? This insightful and stimulating collection of writings by activists, people who work with the young, commentators and young people themselves provides a compelling answer. We need to strike a healthy balance between support and challenge – 'the golden mean'.

16. The Dear Wild Place | *Emily Cutts*
This book recounts the frenetic campaign to protect a magical oasis in the heart of a busy city from housing development – a David and Goliath struggle. Shows how a grassroots initiative can address the intensive materialism of modern life, improve children's lives, provide precious outdoor space for play and health, build a vibrant community and break down barriers caused by pronounced income inequality. An inspiration to all.

17. Play is the Way – Child development, early years and the future of Scottish education | *Sue Palmer (ed)*
Always the Cinderella of the education system, the significance of early years has been seriously under-estimated. **Play is the Way** brings together leading practitioners, policy-makers and academics to explain how a coherent approach to early years – centred on positive relationships and play – will not only result in better educational performance but in greatly improved health and well-being for future Scottish citizens. They challenge the deeply-ingrained cultural acceptance, throughout Scotland and the rest of the UK, that formal instruction in the three Rs (reading, 'riting and 'rithmetic) should begin at the age of four or five – at least a year before other European countries.

More titles are planned for 2021.
Books can be ordered from www.postcardsfromscotland.co.uk or from www.amazon.co.uk Kindle editions are also available for some titles.